6

TREASURY OF TREE LORE

By the same author
Treasury of Bird Lore

TREASURY
OF
TREE
LORE

by
Josephine Addison
and illustrated by
Cherry Hillhouse

ANDRÉ
DEUTSCH

For my husband, Peter

First published in 1999 by
André Deutsch Limited
76 Dean Street
London W1V 5HA
www.vci.co.uk

A Catalogue record for this book is available from the British Library

ISBN 0 233 99437 8

Printed in Great Britain by Jarrold Book Printing, Thetford
Reprographics by Jade Reprographics, Braintree

CONTENTS

ALDER	7		LARCH	84
ALMOND	9		LEMON	87
APPLE	13		LIME	91
APRICOT	17		MEDLAR	95
ASH	20		MULBERRY	98
ASPEN	24		OAK	102
BAY	27		OLIVE	106
BEECH	30		ORANGE	110
BIRCH	33		PEACH	114
BLACKTHORN	36		PEAR	117
BOX	39		SCOTS PINE	121
CEDAR	42		PLANE	125
CYPRESS	45		PLUM	127
ELDER	48		POMEGRANATE	131
ELM	52		ROWAN	134
FIELD MAPLE	56		SYCAMORE	138
FIG	60		TAMARISK	142
HAWTHORN	64		WALNUT	145
HAZEL	68		WILD CHERRY	148
HOLLY	72		WILLOW	151
HORSE CHESTNUT	76		YEW	156
JUNIPER	80		The Laughing Leaves	160

ALDER

I caught the fitful sound
Wafted o'er sullen moss and craggy mound,
Unfruitful solitudes, that seemed to upbraid
The sun in heaven! but now to form a shade
For thee, green alders have together wound
Their foliage.
'Sonnet to Duddon' WILLIAM WORDSWORTH

ALDER (*Alnus glutinosa*). The generic name is the classical Latin word for the tree. Alder and its variants go back beyond Old English. Some etymologists derive the name for this lover of damp habitats from an ancient word for water, *al*. Pollen grains found in peat deposits confirm the alder as a long established tree. It thrives along the banks of rivers and streams throughout Britain, where it not only enriches the soil but helps to prevent its erosion. The male and female catkins grow on the same tree and the green fruits, which ripen in the summer, remain on the tree like tiny dark cones throughout the winter. The alder was often grown in coppices which not only provided shade for stock, particularly for those grazing on mountain slopes, but could also be cut down every nine or ten years to be made into poles.

Homer (800 BC) wrote:

Around it and above for ever green,
The bushy Alders form'd a shady screen.

The wood of the tree is soft but when immersed in water it is extremely durable and was used in the foundations of bridges, for troughs and sluices, and also for water pipes. This inherent quality meant that it was also used for cart and spinning wheels, bowls, spoons, herring barrel staves and even wooden heels.

According to Virgil (70–19 BC) the first boats were built of alder wood:

The rivers first the hollowed Alder knew.

When the wood is young it is brittle and easily worked, but when it is more mature it becomes tinted and veined. It was used in the Highlands of Scotland and known as Scottish mahogany from which rather grand chairs were designed. The branches were used in the production of a good charcoal which was invaluable for making gunpowder, and the bark by tanners, dyers and leather dressers as a foundation for black dyes, and for making fishermen's nets. The leaves have a clammy surface, and spread in a room 'while the morning dew is upon them' they also had a more useful purpose 'ridding the chamber of troublesome bedfellows', i.e. fleas.

In Celtic mythology alder is the tree of the resurrection, marking the emergence of the solar year. The tree was held sacred in some parts of Ireland where it was believed that the burning of one's house followed if the tree was cut down. In the Druidic calendar the fourth or alder month extends from 19 March to 15 April, and includes the spring equinox. In plant lore it typifies fire, from the red of its trunk; water from its green flowers; and earth from the brown of its bark. It is principally a tree of fire and, as a resister of the corruption of water, of the power of fire to free earth from water.

The medicinal properties of the tree were well known to

herbalists. The bark was used as a gargle for sore throats and a compound of the leaf was used to treat burns and inflammations. The leaf could also be applied directly to provide an immediate cooling effect, which was appreciated by weary travellers when applied to their feet.

ALMOND

March is not yet done
Before the solace of a warmer sun
Strokes on our hands and takes us by surprise
With a forgotten touch of naked skin.
The almond breaks to pink against the skies;
Then do we start, and with new-opened eyes
See the true Spring begin.
'The Garden' VITA SACKVILLE-WEST

ALMOND (*Prunus dulcis*). The Greek word *proune,* meaning plum, is the source of the generic name. The almond tree is a native of Western Asia where it was regarded as the sacred tree of life. Nevertheless they have been planted in the Mediterranean regions since ancient times, growing freely in Syria and Palestine and subsequently becoming naturalized in many areas. It is mentioned in the Scriptures several times, for example, 'the almond tree will flourish' in Genesis. The Hebrew word *shakad,* signifying 'to make haste' is an apt name for a tree that flowers in Palestine in January, heralding the awakening of Creation. Legend says the Rod Of Aaron was cut from an almond tree. Jews still carry rods of the blossom to the synagogues on important festivals. The Romans referred to the fruit as Greek nuts; the tree was cultivated in Italy from an early date and the Roman senator and writer, Pliny, mentions almond

amongst a list of Egyptian fruit trees. Although it was grown in France from the eighth century, the Romans most probably introduced almond to England (as it is mentioned in early Anglo-Saxon lists of plants such as the eleventh century 'Durham Glossary', as the 'Easterne nutte-beam', but was not cultivated before 1562. There are early references to the tree in English poetry by writers such as Edmund Spenser (c.1552–1599) in 'The Faerie Queene':

> *Like to an Almond tree ymounted hye,*
> *On top of green Selinis all alone*
> *With blossoms brave bedecked daintly*

The old English name was *almande;* both this name and its modern descendant are from the French word *amande,* derived from the Latin *amandela.* In the anonymous fourth century 'Romance of the Rose' this is the case:

> *And Almandres gret plente.*

William Shakespeare mentions the fruit in *Troilus and Cressida*: 'The parrot will not do more for an Almond.' 'An Almond for a parrot' was a simile in his day for the height of temptation. During the Middle Ages almonds became an important trading commodity in Central Europe and their consumption in medieval cooking was very popular. According to Dorothy Hartley's *Food in England*, a manuscript from 1700 recommends 'Almond butter made with fine sugar and rosewater and eaten with the flower of many violets is a commendable dyshe – specially in lent when Vyolets be fragrant.' The pounded kernels of the nut were used in cakes, puddings, pastries and sauces. Marzipan is probably its best-known form. Almond water was also popular and used much as we use milk today. Old cookery books recommended Jordan Almonds. Sweet almond (*prunus dulcis*) is the variety used for confectionery. The kernel of the bitter almond is the source of the highly poisonous prussic acid, which can of course be safely extracted. A profusion of delicate pink flowers appear before the leaves in early March. This delightful blossom provided a much-needed source of information amongst our ancestors, who regarded various signs of nature as a means of deducing seasonal weather and the quality of the harvest. Virgil wrote:

> *Mark well the flowering Almond in the wood;*
> *If odourous blooms the bearing branches lead,*
> *The glebe will answer to the sylvan reign,*
> *Great heats will follow, and large crops of grain*
> *But if a wood of leaves o'er shade the tree,*
> *Such and so barren will the harvest be.*

The Elizabethan writer and gardener John Gerard informs us that almond trees were 'in our London gardens and orchards in great plenty'. At about the same time the herbalist Culpepper wrote that 'the oil cleanses the skin, it easeth the pain of the chest, the temples being anointed thereof, and the oil with honey, powder of liquorice, oil of roses and white wax, make a good ointment for dimness of sight.' He also recommended almonds with sugar and rose-water, eaten with violets 'for it rejoiceth the heart and comforteth the brain, and qualifieth the heat of the liver'. Sweet almond oil was predominantly used to prepare emulsions, which other herbal remedies have superceded – mainly for cough mixtures. Both sweet and bitter oils are used in cosmetic preparations today.

In Greek legend the almond tree is dedicated to Phyllis, a Thracian princess who, fearing that she had been deserted by her husband Demophon, who had gone to visit his native village, pined away and died. The gods took pity on her and changed her into an almond tree as an eternal compensation for her desertion. When her husband returned and was shown the bare tree, the memorial to his wife, he clasped it in his arms whereupon it burst into bloom – an emblem of true love inextinguishable by death.

Almond is the birthday flower for 8 April with the sentiments being heedlessness, indiscretion and stupidity; it also means the awakener, the first to life in winter, and is a symbol of self-protection, vigilance and both virginity and fruitfulness. The almond in flower signifies hope.

> *The hope in dreams of a happier hour,*
> *That alights on Misery's brow,*
> *Springs out of the silvery Almond flower,*
> *That blooms on a leafless bough*

In 'Pink Almond' Katharine Tynan wrote of the tree's response to cold weather:

> *So delicate so airy*
> *The almond on the tree . . .*
> *A little cloud of roses*
> *All in a world of gray,*
> *The almond flower uncloses*
> *Upon the wild March day.*

Almond and mulberry flowering simultaneously indicates the middle way between hastiness and slowness – the first flowers early, the second late.

APPLE

Is there anything in the Spring so fair,
As apple blossoms falling through the air?
When from the hill there comes a sudden breeze
That blows freshly through all the orchard's trees
The petals drop in clouds of pink and white.
Noiseless like snow and falling in the light.
'Apple Blossoms' HELEN ADAMS PARKER

APPLE (*Malus domestica*). The generic name is the Latin for apple. Many varieties were cultivated from the native wild or crab apple. The name apple was not originally confined to the fruit, but used as a general term, such as in pine-apple and bramble-apple. The crab apple was better known in the sixteenth century than it is today and was served roasted with hot ale – a favourite Christmas dish. This was not for the want of a better fruit because Gerard tells us 'the stocks or kindred of Apples was infinite'. Apple trees were cultivated in monastery gardens during the Middle Ages. In 'Polyolbion' (1613) Michael Drayton lists varieties growing in the Kentish orchards, including the 'pippen', which applied, at that time to any apple raised from a pip:

> *The pippen, which we hold of kernl fruits the king;*
> *The apple orange; then the savoury russetan;*
> *The permain, which to France long erer to us 'twas known,*
> *Which careful fruiterers now have denizen'd our own;*
> *The renat, which though at first it from the pippen came*
> *Grown through its pureness nice, assumes that curious name;*
> *The sweeting, for whose sake the schoolboys oft make war,*
> *The wilding, costard, then the well known pomewater,*
> *And sundry other fruits of good yet several taste.*
> *And have their sundry names in sundry counties placed.*

In plant lore apple blossom is the birthday flower for 31 December, signifying preference. In the language of the flowers it means; 'He prefers you' but can also mean 'Fame called him great and good'. As a herald of May it is appropriate to brides. An apple tree symbolizes youthful beauty and frequently figures as a tree of everlasting youth, and also as one of knowledge or life. The superstitious believed that apple blossom appearing in the autumn, particularly on the same branch as the fruit, foretold the death of the owner's family. Hence the couplet:

> *A bloom on the tree when the Apples are ripe,*
> *Is a sure termination to somebody's life.*

It was equally dangerous to leave an apple on the tree after the harvest, although in some parts of Britain it was considered unlucky to remove them all, as some should be left as a gift for the fairies and sprites. There were those that believed that if the sun shone through the apple trees on Christmas morning – others say Easter – it was a sign of a good crop and a prosperous year for the owner. An ancient ceremony also helped and was celebrated on New Year's Eve or Twelfth Night; people would assemble with great revelry, noisily beating pans, kettles and trays in their local orchard, while impressively armed with jugs of cider. One tree was chosen and cider-soaked bread was fastened to it and the jugs' contents poured over the roots and then down the throats of the revellers. As an extra precaution,

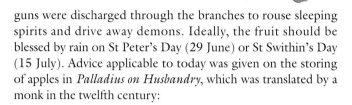

guns were discharged through the branches to rouse sleeping spirits and drive away demons. Ideally, the fruit should be blessed by rain on St Peter's Day (29 June) or St Swithin's Day (15 July). Advice applicable to today was given on the storing of apples in *Palladius on Husbandry*, which was translated by a monk in the twelfth century:

> *Lay them dark as wind may not come near,*
> *And do fair straw upon them fleyke them under,*
> *Or in heaps save, a little space asunder.*

A popular Hallowtide game, which was actually a love divination ceremony, was played with each person whirling round an apple on a string in front of the fire. The first apple to fall indicated a marriage and the last signified that the owner would die unwed. To gauge the depth of a lover's feelings apple pips were arranged on the bars of the fireplace and the following words spoken:

> *If you love me, bounce and fly,*
> *If you hate me, lie and die.*

If the pip burst noisily, the lover was faithful, but if not the pip quietly burnt away. As with many superstitions a variation held that a silent burning foretold a smooth courtship with a happy ending and the reverse applied to a bursting pip. Girls would also press the pips on their cheeks, giving a name to each one, the pip that stayed on the longest indicating the identity of their future husband. An alternative ceremony was to peel an apple in one long strip and throw it over the left shoulder, where it would form the initial of one's future spouse on the ground.

In lore the apple is a symbol of fruitfulness, health, knowledge, love and wisdom but also death, discord, evil, lust and temptation. In witchcraft it is the food of the oracular dead and in fairy tales the giver of immortal youth. In the Christmas tradition it signifies earthly happiness, fruit of the Tree of Knowledge of Good and Evil. It symbolizes the fall of man and original sin. In the hands of Adam, weakness; in the hands of

Eve, damnation; in the hands of Jesus, the new Adam; in the hands of Mary, the new Eve, redemption or salvation.

Everyone is familiar with the old saying 'An apple a day keeps the doctor away' but there are several superstitions associated with the medicinal virtues of the fruit. Our ancestors believed that to eat one large apple at midnight on Halloween would prevent a cold year. An unusual cure for warts, for which there seem to have been numerous remedies, required the fruit to be halved and each portion rubbed on the wart before the halves were tied together and buried – as the fruit rotted away the wart would disappear.

Numerous recipes for cider, butter, jellies, cheese, puddings and tarts have survived the centuries, including one in the form of a long poem by a Mr King, entitled the 'Ancestral Apple Pie', which begins with the following verse:

Of all the delicates which Britons try
To please the palate or delight the eye,
Of all the several kinds of sumptuous fare,
There is none that can with applepie compare.
Honour and fame alike we will partake
So well I'll eat what you so richly make

APRICOT

Would I were,
For all the fortunes of my life hereafter,
Yon little tree, yon blooming Apricocke;
How I would spread and fling my wanton armes
In at her window! I would bring her fruit
Fit for the gods to feed on.
'The Noble Kinsmen' WILLIAM SHAKESPEARE

APRICOT (*Prunus armeniaca*). The apricot is sometimes thought to have come from Armenia although there is little doubt it originated in the Himalayan region. The common name is from the Latin *praecox*, or *praecoquus*, which was used by the Roman writer Pliny. It has since been subjected to various continental interpretations. It acquired the name 'precocious tree' because it flowered and fruited earlier than the peach, as Lyte explained in his *Herbal* of 1578: 'There be two kinds of Peaches, whereof the one kinde is late ripe . . . the other kinds are soner ripe, wherefore they be called Abrecox or Aprecox.'

The time of the introduction of the tree into England is somewhat vague, although in 1548 William Turner, regarded as the father of British botany, wrote 'we have very few of these trees as yet'. However, Richard Hakluyt stated that it was brought from Italy by a man named Wolf, a gardener to Henry VIII, and the apricot would seem to have been grown as a standard in William Shakespeare's time. Advice on pruning the tree is given by the bard in *Richard II* when he writes on a seemingly bountiful crop:

Go, bind thou up yon dangling Apricocks,
Which, like unruly children, make their sire
Stoop with oppression of their prodigal weight:

> *Give some supportance to the bending twigs.*
> *Go thou, like an executioner,*
> *Cut off the heads of too-fast growing sprays.*

Similarly, in *Britannia's Pastorals* William Browne wrote:

> *Or if from where he is he do espy*
> *Some Apricot upon a bough thereby*
> *Which overhangs the tree on which he stands,*
> *Climbs up, and strives to take them with his hands.*

Climatic changes over the centuries cause the horticulturist of today to advise that the tree be planted in a sunny sheltered position – ideally against a wall or in a greenhouse – in order to protect the blossom from frost and low temperatures in late winter and early spring. As apricots are self-fertile, they have to be pollinated by hand in cool areas. Although the fan-shaped method – whereby two branches radiate out from twelve inches above the ground, with the central stem removed (otherwise the growth becomes too vigorous near the top) – is decorative, and requires regular pruning in spring and autumn, it does enable the fruit to receive maximum sunlight.

Apricots ripen in late July and early August according to the variety. They were imported in large quantities and the kernels of several varieties are edible. As they contain constituents similar to those of bitter almonds they were used by confectioners as a substitute. The French liqueur Eau de Noyaux is prepared from bitter apricot kernels. Apricot oil was often used as an alternative for Oil of Almonds (which it closely resembles), or just added to the oil in the manufacture of almond-based soaps and creams. Today, however, it is used in its own right.

In earlier times fruit-stuffed hams, baked and wrapped in a crust, were very popular at the annual wool fairs and sheep-shearing suppers. Apricots, used as a basis for the stuffing (with the stones removed) were mixed with an equal quantity of white bread crumbs, pepper and salt and lightly cooked in a little water until the juices ran. After the baked ham had cooled the crust was removed. Apricot kernels were then cracked and splintered over the sugar-glazed ham. Old cookery books abound with recipes of tarts, compotes, puddings, iced eggs, preserves and wine and advice on drying and storage which testifies to the popularity of the fruit. In plant lore the fruit signifies nympha and also vulva. The flower is a symbol of timid love.

ASH

We sought the hollow ash that was shelter from the rain
With our pockets full of pease we had stolen from the grain
How delicious was the dinner time on such a showery day
O words are poor receipts for what time hath stole away
The ancient pulpit trees and the play.
'Remembrances' JOHN CLARE

COMMON ASH (*Fraxinus excelsior*). The generic name comes from the Latin word *frango* (I break), denoting the ease with which it may be split. Nevertheless, because of its strength it was used for spear shafts, and the Anglo-Saxon *aesc* (ash) came to mean spear, and *aesc-plega*, the game of spears, a battle. Ash wood, which is almost pure white and very pliable, is used for the handles of various tools, such as axes and hammers, but also for oars and sporting equipment. Advice on the ash as a fuel is given in an old rhyming proverb:

Burn Ash-wood green
'Tis a fire for a queen;
Burn Ash-wood sear,
'Twill make a man swear.

It is usually found growing on good land, which gave rise to an old saying: 'May your footfall be by the root of an ash tree.' In weather lore throughout Britain the ash has always been associated with the oak:

When buds the oak before the ash,
You'll only have a summer splash

When the oak comes out before the ash, there will be fine weather in harvest; but when the ash comes out before the oak, the harvest will be wet:

When the ash is out before the oak,
Then expect a choke [drought]
When the oak is out before the ash,
Then we may expect a splash.

A briefer old saying, 'Oak choke, ash splash', meant that if the oak came into leaf first, dry, dusty weather would follow, but if the ash was first, rainy weather was to come. The last word must go to a correspondent to *Notes and Queries*, in 1873 who wrote to say that he never knew the ash to come into leaf before the oak!

The Scottish poet David Gray (1835–61) was mindful of the signs and sounds of spring when he wrote 'To A Friend':

Now, while long delaying ash assumes
The delicate April green, and, loud and clear,
Through the cool, yellow mellow twighlight glooms,
The thrush's sung enchants the captive ear.

In plant lore the ash is the birthday emblem for 27 December with the sentiment of grandeur; in the language of the flowers it means 'With me you are safe.' It is symbolic of adaptability, flexibility, modesty and nobility. It is a tree of good omen

emblematic of fire and man. The ancients believed the ash possessed magical powers which averted the evil eye. It was used as a charm against drowning and believed to have power over the sea and for this reason oars were made from it. The Vikings in particular favoured the wood for boat building. As a prevention against drowning, witches' broomsticks were made of ash – the birch twigs being bound with willow. The five magic trees whose fall in medieval poetry symbolized the triumph of Christianity over paganism were ash trees. In Northern Europe the ash was generally considered sacred and therefore protective and for this reason was planted around the home. A leaf with an even number of leaflets was called an even-ash, and was used in love divination ceremonies:

> *The even-Ash-leaf in my hand*
> *The first I meet shall be my man.*

If a girl slept with the leaf under her pillow her future husband would appear, whether he was married or not at the time. On Christmas Eve the burning of ashen-faggots – ash twigs bound with ash – was a popular fire charm ceremony; single girls would pick one of the bands and the first one to burst in the heat of the fire indicated a marriage. In *Brand's Popular Antiquities* of 1797 a poem alludes to this old custom:

> *. . . nine bandages it bears,*
> *And as they disjoin (as custom wills),*
> *A mighty jug of cyder's brought*

Passing a child through a split in an ash sapling was the magical treatment for a hernia and rickets while bed wetting was said to be cured by the afflicted child gathering ash keys which would then be burnt on the hearth. The cure was effected by the child urinating on the ashes. Whooping cough was cured by pinning a lock of the patient's hair to an ash tree. In some parts of England April and May were considered to be the best months for curing children's warts. One of the parents carried a packet of new pins to the tree, pressing a pin into the bark and then into the child's wart until it caused pain, and then back into the bark. Alternatively one could cross the wart three times with a pin – after each crossing this charm was spoken:

Ashen tree, Ashen tree,
Pray buy this wart off me.

Herbalists in the thirteenth century recommended ash keys, boiled in the patient's urine, soaked in black wool as a cure for ulcerated ears – the words, 'By God's help, it will cure it' were beneficial too. In Roman mythology ash is assigned to Mars, god of war. And in Greek mythology the magical spear which Chiron gave to Peleus was made of the wood. It had the power to heal those it wounded but was so huge that only Achilles could wield it. The ash is perhaps better known in Norse mythology as the tree dedicated to Odin, the chief god, and named Yggdrasil, the Tree of Life. It represented the universe on a small scale and by its roots were three primitive wells. In its branches lived Idun, the goddess of life, and the three weird sisters of fate, the past and the present and future, who sprinkled the tree with pure water so that it would not wither. An eagle, a squirrel and a hawk also lived in the branches and a serpent in the roots; a goat which fed on the leaves gave milk to the heroes of Valhalla, the Nordic heaven. Under the tree stood a horn which would one day blow to announce the end of the universe.

ASPEN

There are the aspens, with their silvery leaves
Trembling, for ever trembling;
though the lime
And chestnut boughs, and those long
arching sprays
Of eglantine, hang still, as if the wood
Was all one picture.
'Wood-walk and Hymn' FELICIA HEMANS

ASPEN (*Populus tremula*). Named from the Latin *populus*, the tree of the people, and according to an anonymous old writer 'its readily moved and ever-stirring leaves were, like the ever restless multitude, quickened into action by the slightest breath.' Country names for the aspen include trembling poplar, old wives' tongue, shaking asp and pipple. This beautiful tree, found throughout Britain, produces male and female catkins on separate trees, and has leaves which change to varying shades of amber in the autumn. Its Latin name comes because the leaves quiver in the slightest breeze, due entirely to the flattening of the long stalk on which they grow.

Alfred, Lord Tennyson noted their gentle movements in 'The Lady of Shalott':

Willows whiten, aspens quiver,
Little breezes dusk and shiver
Thro' the wave that runs for ever
By the island in the river
Flowing down to Camelot.

The constant movement of the foliage was 'likened to the unceasing course of time' although some of our ancestors had a different explanation. In the Christian tradition it is a tree of

mourning, pride and sinful arrogance. According to one legend all the trees bowed their heads when Jesus was crucified, with one exception:

But one tree in the forest
That refused to bow;
Then a sudden blast came o'er it,
And a whisper low
Made the leaves and branches quiver –
Shook the guilty tree;
And the voice was, 'Tremble ever
To eternity'

The poem, signed 'FCW', was published in *Chambers' Journal* and concludes with the following lines:

So thou standest ever shaking
Ever quivering with fear
And thy leaves are thoughts and doubtings
For thou art the sinner's tree.

Another legend suggests that the cross on which Christ was crucified was made of aspen wood and thereafter the aspen trembled. Felicia Hemans wrote:

> *To the strange restlessness of those wan leaves;*
> *The cross, he deems, the blessed cross, whereon*
> *The meek Redeemer bowed His head to death,*
> *Was formed of Aspen wood.*

Aspen was synonymous with female loquacity, as the following verse from *The Schoole-house of Women* shows:

> *The Aspin lefe hanging where it be,*
> *With little winde or none it shaketh;*
> *A woman's tung in like wise taketh*
> *Little ease and little rest;*
> *For if it should the hart would brest.*

The herbalist John Gerard concludes his account of the tree with the lines 'In English Aspe and Aspen tree, and may also be called Tremble, after the French name, considering it is the matter whereof women's tongues were made (as the poets and some others report), which seldom cease wagging.' Today, 'to tremble like a leaf' is a common enough expression.

Herbalists long regarded the aspen as a cure for ague and in *Folklore of the Northern Counties*, Henderson refers to a girl pinning a lock of hair to a tree.

> *Aspen tree, aspen tree*
> *I prithee to shake and shiver instead of me.*

This was a form of sympathetic magic whereby like cured like. If the girl returned home in complete silence she was supposedly cured. Alternatively, a piece of fingernail was pressed into the bark of the tree and as the bark grew over it, the complaint slowly faded away. The somewhat astringent bark was used as a tonic, for fevers and as a diuretic in urinary infections and gonorrhoea.

During the reign of Henry V an Act of Parliament was passed to prevent the use of the tree other than for making arrows, with a penalty of a 'Hundred shillings if used for making pattens or clogs'.

In plant lore aspen signifies excessive sensibility, fear (due to its quivering leaves), lamentation and scandal.

BAY

SWEET BAY (*Laurus nobilis*). The generic name is Latin for laurel (not to be confused with the large-leaved laurel) and regarded as a curious instance of the capriciousness of English plant names – it is a true laurel, but does not bear its name. Alternative ones, however, include Roman laurel, poet's laurel, true laurel, noble laurel, lorer and daphne. Originally from northern Asia, bay is now widely distributed throughout Europe and the Mediterranean regions. Today, this evergreen, which produces yellowish-green flowers in the spring and oval black berries in the autumn, can be seen as an attractive and valuable addition in herb gardens and clipped to decorative designs in ornamental pots both in town and country.

In Greek mythology bay is an attribute of Apollo, the son of Zeus, who fell in love with Daphne, the daughter of a river god. As she had sworn to spend her life a virgin she rejected him. To escape his ardent advances Daphne asked her father for protection and he changed her into a bay tree. Apollo declared from that day he would wear bay instead of oak and all

those who sought his favour, should do likewise:

> *The bay Apollo! With dark leaf is thine,*
> *Thus art thou honour'd at the Delphic shrine*

wrote Theocritus. Bay was used in garlands and crowns for
poetic elegance or victory in battle and the Greeks awarded
their champions at the Pythian Games a wreath of bay. It was
held in great esteem by physicians and regarded as the cure for
all ailments, so much so that the statue of the god of medicine,
Asculepius, was adorned with a wreath of its leaves. Older writers always referred to bay in the plural and said that it was 'not
subject to any hurt of Jupiter's thunderbolts' as other trees are:

> *Where bayes still grow (by thunder not struck down)*
> *The victor's garland and the poet's crown.*

It was generally believed that if bay was planted close to the
house 'neither witch nor devil, thunder or lightening will hurt
a man where the bay tree is'. Later a Jacobean dramatist
advised:

> *Reach the bays*
> *I'll tie a garland here about his head*
> *I will keep my boy from lightening*

The emperor Tiberius, who was said to be frightened of thun-
derstorms, crouched under his bed during storms, clutching
boughs of the plant to preserve his life. He and other Roman

emperors wore a wreath of bay as an amulet and during Saturnalia, a pagan forerunner of Christmas, decorated their homes with the leaves. This delightful custom, described in *Hazlitt's Popular Poetry*, has survived using other evergreens to this day:

> *Spread out the laurel and the bay*
> *For chimney-piece and window gay,*
> *Scour the brass gear – a shining row*
> *And holly place with Mistletoe.*

The withering of a bay tree was a bad omen and it is claimed that before the death of Emperor Nero all the bay trees in Rome are said to have died.

Shakespeare wrote:

> *'Tis thought the King is dead; we will not stay.*
> *The bay-trees in our country are all wither'd.*

He was thought to have copied this superstition from an Italian source, because this was not a sign in England of impending calamity. However, Shakespeare does make a more familiar culinary reference in *Pericles*:

> *'Marry come up, my dish of chastity and with Rosemary and Bays.'*

The chief dish at feasts and banquets was thus decorated. John Parkinson (1567–1650) was full of praise for the tree: 'the bay leaves are of as necessary use as any other in the garden or orchard, for they serve both for pleasure and profit, both for ornament and use, both for honest civil uses and for physic. . .'

In plant lore bay is the birthday flower for 14 July with the sentiment of everlasting attraction. A bay berry signifies discipline and instruction while a bay leaf in the language of the flowers means 'I change only in death.'

BEECH

> *... thou, light wingèd Dryad*
> *of the trees*
> *In some melodious plot*
> *Of beechen green, and*
> *shadows numberless,*
> *Singest of summer in*
> *full-throated ease.*
> 'Ode to a Nightingale'
> JOHN KEATS

BEECH (*Fagus sylvatica*).
The generic name *fagus* is Latin for beech while *sylvatica* means growing in woodlands. The branches provide an airy, latticed space in spring for carpets of bluebells and wood anemones fringed with primroses to flourish in a glorious profusion of colour before the delicate pale green leaves unfurl, forming a protective canopy which prevents further growth on the ground with the possible exception of fungi. At the same time the extensive root system helps to sustain the surrounding soil.

> *Its long thin buds in glistering varnish dipt*
> *Are swinging up and down*
> *While one young beech that winter left unstript*
> *Still wears its withered crown.*

The earliest runes were written on beech board; the Anglo-Saxon word *bece* meant book and beech. The 'nuts' of the beech, known as 'masts' (formerly 'bucks', from which the county of Buckinghamshire, famous for its beech woods, takes its name). Masts were used as fodder for deer and in some countries for domestic animals, with the exception of horses.

Inside the four-valved husk are two triangular nutlets.

Beech is one of the largest British trees and is a truly splendid sight when mantled in its summer finery, supported by its distinctive smooth grey trunk. The beech has its roots very firmly in the past and is thought to have been here long before Britain became an island. While never having the reputation of the oak as a building material it has always been used extensively as a fuel – it was used in Roman times when mixed beech woods supplied the fuel for iron works. It was also used extensively for the keels of sailing ships, galley oars, piles and floodgates, granary shovels, stonemason's mallets, panels for carriages, parquet flooring and small pieces of turnery, and later, when Bentwood and Windsor furniture became popular, for chairs. Chairmakers known as 'bodgers' often worked within the woods setting up simple lathes to turn the legs.

Abraham Cowley wrote:

Hence in the world's best years the humble shed
Was happily and fully furnished.
Beech made their chests, their beds, and their join'd stools:
Beech made the boards, the platters, and the bowls.

Beech not only provided containers for food and drink but chips of the wood were used to clarify wine. Cowley also wrote:

He sings to Bacchus, patron of the vine,
The beechen bowl, foams with a flood of wine.

The heating power of beech was said to surpass all other wood, and according to an old adage the felling of the tree was of great significance because it was alleged that if this occurred about Midsummer, the wood would last three times longer than if it was felled in winter.

Beech in Summer
Oak in Winter.

Groves and avenues of the tree reflect the grandeur of their past. The same applies to hedges of young beech, which are popular today in flower gardens, particularly as they not only

retain their leaves, for the most part, throughout the year, but protect plants and maintain privacy during the winter months. One magnificent hedge with an historical connection can be found in Scotland. It is said that while it was being planted in 1745 the workmen heard that Bonnie Prince Charles had landed. They immediately stopped work, only returning a year later to complete the task. It is now a famous landmark.

The superstitious used the tree to forecast the weather, suggesting that when beech masts thrive well and oak trees hang full, a hard winter will follow, wth much snow. When beech nuts are plentiful expect a mild winter. If on All Saints' Day (1 November) the beech nut is dry, we shall have a hard winter; but if the nut is wet expect a wet winter. If the tree displays large buds at about Christmas there will be a probability of a moist season the succeeding summer.

Beech leaves collected in the autumn before the frosts were said to make an excellent stuffing for mattresses – lasting seven or eight years, giving, one presumes, in the early stages at least, 'a fragrant odour like that of green tea'. The catkins were used for a similar purpose and also for packing fruit.

Herbalists used the water collected from the hollows of the trees to soothe sores, scabs and scurf on man and animals and because of their coolness, fresh leaves were applied to hot swellings. Boiled leaves were used as a poultice and as an ointment. Oil extracted from the nut formed the basis of an expectorant in the treatment of bronchitis and was applied externally as a treatment for various skin complaints.

BIRCH

SILVER BIRCH (*Betula pendula*). The generic name is the Latin word for birch. It is one of two native to the British Isles, the other being downy birch, and was one of the first trees to re-establish itself after the glacial period. It has a slender silvery colour and possesses a lightness and grace about its branches and fluttering triangular leaves, which after rain exude a fragrant odour. Coleridge referred to it as:

The most beautiful
Of forest tree, the lady of the wood.

In winter a reddish haze seems to enhance the branches which are decked in April with pale green female and purple-brown male catkins. Despite its delicate appearance it is one of the hardiest trees in the world, thriving in barren windswept landscapes and mountainous regions. Our ancestors made great use of the tree; the protuberances on the birch, known as witch's knobs, were carved into bowls and the wood was used for house

building, furniture (particularly chairs), fences, ploughs, stakes and broom handles. Later, as the wood was cheap and pliable, it was used for bobbins in the booming thread mills and for herring barrel staves. The branches were used in distilling whisky, smoking ham and herrings, for thatching house roofs, wattle fencing, for broom heads and as charcoal in forges. Birch charcoal was used in the manufacture of gunpowder. The bark of the tree was separated into thin layers and used as a substitute for oiled paper. It was also one of the materials on which the ancients wrote. According to Pliny, the celebrated books of Numa Pompilius, compiled 700 years before the birth of Christ, and burned with their author, were written on birch bark. A resinous extraction known commercially as Oil of Birch Tar was used in the dressing process of leather. Allegedly, it prevented mould forming on books and kept insects at bay. A pleasant but very potent wine can be prepared from the thin sugary sap of the tree by tapping in March. Fermentation takes place with the addition of yeast, honey, cloves and lemon peel.

The superstitious believed that the dwarf birch is stunted because it was used to scourge Jesus Christ. The poet David Gray, however, having dug one up in Garstone Woods, thought that they were just as beautiful as their elegant relatives:

> *I plucked a little Birchen tree*
> *The spongy moss adorning;*
> *And bearing it delighted home,*
> *I planted it in garden loam,*
> *Where, perfecting all duty,*
> *It flowered in tasselled beauty.*

In ancient times the Romans used birch rods during the installation of their consuls, considering the birch a tree of inception. In England, because it was thought to have sacred powers of renewal and purification, birch rods were used to drive out the spirits of the old year. The Scots, however, associated the tree with the dead, particularly with ghosts. As late as the nineteenth century it was customary on the Feast of the Holy Innocents (28 December) to beat boys with birch twigs in a ritualistic reminder of the children murdered by King Herod. In *Measure for Measure* Shakespeare wrote of a more common use:

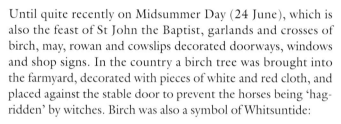

> *Now, as fond fathers,*
> *Having bound up the*
>   *threatening twigs of birch,*
> *Only to stick it in their childrens sight*
> *For terror, not to use, do find in time*
> *The rod more mocked than fear'd.*

Until quite recently on Midsummer Day (24 June), which is also the feast of St John the Baptist, garlands and crosses of birch, may, rowan and cowslips decorated doorways, windows and shop signs. In the country a birch tree was brought into the farmyard, decorated with pieces of white and red cloth, and placed against the stable door to prevent the horses being 'hag-ridden' by witches. Birch was also a symbol of Whitsuntide:

> *When Yew is out and Birch comes in,*
> *And many flowers beside*
> *Both of fresh and fragrant kin*
> *To honour Whitsuntide*

wrote Robert Herrick in 'Candlemas Eve'. A broomstick or besom wedding was once held to be legal. A couple who wished to dispense with formalities simply jumped over a birch broom held against the doorway of the house and were married.

Herbalists used the juice of the leaves, which are said to have an aromatic, agreeable odour and bitter taste, as a remedy for kidney stones and as a mouthwash. More recently birch leaves were used in the treatment of eczema. An infusion (birch tea) was recommended for gout, rheumatism and dropsy.

Astrologically, birch is under the dominion of Venus and is the birthday emblem for 14 April, with the sentiments being grace and meekness. In the language of the flowers it means 'You may begin' and was given by a girl to a young man as a sign of encouragement.

BLACKTHORN

Wanton with long delay, the gay spring leaping cometh;
The blackthorn starreth now his boughs on the eve of May:
All day in the sweet box-tree the bee for pleasure hummeth:
The cuckoo sends afloat his note in the air all day.
'April' ROBERT BRIDGES

BLACKTHORN (*Prunus spinosa*). The generic name is Latin for plum. The common name probably derives from the colour of the bark which is darker than the hawthorn. Blackthorn, which is known as sloe, is a large thorny shrub and occasionally a small tree, native throughout the British Isles. It is one of the wild ancestors of our many varieties of plums. In early spring the dainty white flowers, with their coral anthers, appear on the spiky branches before the leaves. As they sometimes appear following a mild spell in early March, which can be a time of cold east winds accompanied by snow, the period is known as a 'blackthorn winter'.

The blue-black fruit, known as sloes or bullace, can be made into a strongly flavoured wine. The whole fruit is packed into a bottle topped up with gin and a dash of brandy, corked and stored in a warm dark cupboard. The result is a delicious liqueur known as sloe gin. When sloes are used for this purpose they are better picked after the first frost, which bursts the skin slightly. Previously blended with penny royal and valerian, sloe gin was used by country wives 'in connubial emergencies' (hence the name 'Mother's Ruin'). Traditionally sloes were bottled in the autumn and buried deep in the earth to be brought out at Christmas and eaten as a preserve. Sloes were also a standard medicine for cow flux.

Thomas Tusser (c.1524–1580) advised his readers on their storage:

By the end of October go gather up Sloes,
Have thou in readiness plentie of thoes,
And keepe them in bed-straw, or still on the bow,
To staie both the flix of thy selfe and the cow.

During the nineteenth century the sloe acquired a rather dubious reputation as the juice was used to make a 'port wine'. Many superstitions are associated with the fruit:

Many sloes, many groans

goes the old saying signifying a hard winter to follow, likely to cause poverty and even death. Another saying is:

Many sloes, many cold toes.

One proverb, 'as black as a sloe', was a popular comparison and 'as useless as a sloe', or 'not worth a sloe', was as common. In plant lore blackthorn is symbolic of difficulty and ill luck. In the Celtic alphabet it is the tree of the sixth consonant, and it shares the month of the willow from 16 April to 13 May, the month in which Good Friday falls. In Christian legend the crown of thorns was said to have been the blackthorn, a reason given by monks, who considered it unlucky, to bring a spray of the flowers into the home and to this day many people feel the same way. Formerly a New Year decoration, it was fashioned in the form of a wreath, scorched over a fire and decorated with mistletoe. It was later used as a fertility offering when it was taken out in the spring to the fields and burnt, with the ashes scattered over the earliest sown wheat.

Since the wood is limited in size it was used for the teeth of hay-rakes, in marquetry, and for cudgels and walking sticks. Blackthorn staves were indispensable in the rough game of quarterstaff. Witches were believed to carry a blackthorn rod with which they were said to cause miscarriages and, as a consequence, they were burnt with them.

The herbalist William Coles advised that as the fruit and bark were astringent blackthorn was good for bleeding, diarrhoea, swellings, infected wounds and 'gripings and gnawings in the stomach'.

A tisane of blackthorn blossoms was recommended as a gentle laxative which 'purges to the depths' and as a means of purifying the blood of children with 'skin eruptions'. Sucking a sloe was said to cure gumboils although Culpepper suggested that 'the sloe is not fit to be eaten until the autumn frosts mellow them' and that 'leaves make lotions to gargle the mouth and throat, wherein swelling sores, or kernels; to stay the defluction of rheum to the eyes, or other parts; and to cool the heat and inflammations of them, and ease hot pains of the head, to bathe the forehead and temples therewith.' The dusty black bark of the tree was also the basis of medieval ink.

Box

And in the scent of box on genial day
When sun is warm as seldom in this isle,
Smell something of the South, as clippings pile
Beneath your tread, like aromatic spray
Strewn down the paving of cathedral aisle
On pagan-Christian feast-day, for the feet
Of the devout to crush.
'The Garden' VITA SACKVILLE-WEST

BOX (*Buxus sempervirens*). The generic name is the Latin name of the tree, derived from *semper*, always and *vovo*, alive, alluding to the tenacity of the plant. *Buxus* also denotes a flute – the wood was prized for making musical instruments. It is a native tree which in the past often grew to a considerable size, evidence of which can be found in Box Hill in Surrey. Today it is more likely to be a small rounded one, often the size of a large bush, or a dense evergreen hedge, with shiny dark green leaves. For the artistically inclined, box can be fashioned, sometimes using a frame, and clipped into a splendid shape, the art of which is known as topiary. The dwarf variety, known as 'edging box', was originally used to form borders round graves and during the Elizabethan period it was used in attractive knot gardens – small intricate beds of flowers or herbs. In recent times this gardening fashion has enjoyed a renaissance. In her charming long poem 'The Garden' Vita Sackville-West advised:

Plant box for edging; do not heed the glum
Advice of those unthinking orthodox
Gardeners who condemn the tidy box
As a haven for the slug . . . and with August come
Clip neatly (you may also clip in May
If time allow, a double yearly trim
To make your edging thicker and more prim).

The custom of clipping dwarf box in topiary gardening is said to have originated with the Romans.

Box is a delicate yellow, hard and beautifully grained wood and because it does not warp, was used as blocks for wood engraving, marquetry, for chess pieces and mathematical instruments. Gerard described the root as 'a timber of greater beauty and more fit for dagger haftes, boxes and suchlike. Turners and cuttlers do call this wood Dudgeon, wherewith they make Dudgeon-hafted daggers.' The Romans are believed to have cultivated box on English hillsides for their civic and religious ceremonies. Chaucer noted it as a dismal tree and in *The Knight's Tale*, he describes Palamon in his misery as:

Like was he to byholde
The Boxe tree or the Asschen deed and colde

Henry Ellacombe observed that box could be 'cut and tortured into ungainly shapes which so delighted our ancestors in Shakespeare's time, though one of the most illustrious of them, Bacon, entered his protest against such barbarism.' He thought they were only suitable for children! The trees at that time must have been quite large because in *Twelfth Night* one finds:

Get ye all three into the Box tree.

Boughs of box were gathered on Candlemas Eve (1 February) for the decoration of churches and the fireplace in the home. Robert Herrick wrote on replacing the Christmas decorations:

Instead of Holly now upraise
The greener Box for show

Formerly box was used instead of willow on Palm Sunday. The Domesday Book records that a tenant rendered a bundle of box-twigs as part of his payment for that religious festival.

In plant lore it is the birthday flower for 17 September, and is a symbol of grace, prosperity and stoicism; it bears the sentiment 'tattling' – given to idle talk. Its tell-tale leaves, when crushed in the hand, will, with their crackling sound, reveal the truth to a lover. Box has a long history and is mentioned by Isaiah in the Bible. In ancient Rome it was sacred to Mercury, the messenger of the gods, but the ancient Greeks venerated it as a funeral or shrine tree. This association with death was perpetuated in the north of England as late as the nineteenth century, when it was customary for the mourners to take a piece of the shrub as a symbol of remembrance. When the coffin was lowered into the grave, they filed past, dropping in their evergreen token. Wordsworth recalled the burial of a child:

> *The basin of Box-wood, just six months before,*
> *Had stood on the table at Timothy's door;*
> *A coffin through Timothy's thresh-hold has passed*
> *One child did it bear, and that child was his last.*

This rather moving tradition continues today with the sweet-scented rosemary, also used in the past, or a favourite flower.

Box leaves, which are said to have a nauseous taste, were powdered and used as an excellent vermifuge. Various extracts and perfumes were made from the bark and leaves. Mixed with sawdust boiled in lye, they were used as an auburn-coloured hair dye. The leaves, dried and powdered, are highly poisonous but were administered with great care to horses; to improve their coats and to treat worms. In former times box was an active ingredient in the remedy for the bite of a mad dog. It is surprising, therefore, to learn that animals seldom eat it.

In medieval times cooks used the leaves as a decorative motif, in the form of a *fleur-de-lis.* Six leaves, three large and three small, formed the heraldic device arranged with a gilded clove on an earlier version of gingerbread – more of a slab than a cake). It was a popular gift during tournaments.

CEDAR

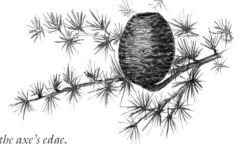

Thus yields the Cedars to the axe's edge,
Whose arms gave shelter to the princely eagle,
Under whose shade the ramping lion slept,
Whose top-branches o'erpeered Jove's spreading tree,
And kept low shrubs from winter's powerful wind.
Henry IV, Part II WILLIAM SHAKESPEARE

CEDAR OF LEBANON (*Cedrus libani*). The generic name is of Arabic origin, via Greek, from *kedron* or *kedros*, meaning power. It was introduced to Britain as a rather splendid ornamental tree although accounts vary regarding the date of its introduction. John Evelyn tried to cultivate the tree but did not at first succeed and it is not mentioned in his *Sylva* of 1664. However, by 1676 it appears in the gardener's accounts of Bretby Park, Derbyshire and in 1683 a cedar was planted in Chelsea Botanic Gardens. Since that time it has proved so suitable to the English soil and climate that it is grown everywhere – providing there is enough space. Capability Brown, with his masterly touch in landscape gardening on a grand scale, favoured this magnificent tree as he swept through England re-designing the larger formal gardens and parks of the landed gentry. As the cedar is slow growing and long-lived the plantings undertaken in the eighteenth and nineteenth century still grace the countryside today. The cones, which ripen in two years, are very distinctive, large and oval. They perch upright on the horizontal branches, releasing their seeds to the winds. In ancient times the Eygptians used the wood of the Lebanon cedar to build their temples. Solomon lined the Temple at Jerusalem with sweet cedar wood. It was all 'carved with knops and open flowers.' Inside its solid walls 'all was cedar, there was no stone to see' (Kings vi, 18). He also built himself a palace of

cedar-wood in the centre of the forest of Lebanon. He is also said to have raised three temples, in which he used cedar and fir, to honour a Trinity composed of Jehovah and two birth or fertility goddesses. One story tells of the Queen of Sheba, on a visit to King Solomon, being invited to cross a bridge of cedar wood built over some marshy ground. As she was about to do so, she had a vision that the wood would bear the sacred body of the Saviour of the world and so she refused to cross. Another legend tells of the angel who took shelter from a storm beneath a cedar tree. The storm abated and the angel asked God that this fragrant, shady tree should bear fruit to benefit the human race. The fruit was the sacred body of Christ. The sweet-scented resin distilled from the wood was used as an embalming agent to preserve the bodies of their dead:

> … *the agelong, spicy strength*
> *Of the Lebanon cedars, shimmering with needles,*
> *and stout*
> *With their perching cones. And Solomon passed to*
> *his rest.*

In the Christian tradition the cedar is an emblem of Christ, and in the Jewish faith it is a symbol of fragrance, empire and nobility. Vita Sackville-West wrote:

> *Is it to Lebanon that looks across*
> *To Palestine and throws the cedar shade*
> *To touch the greater shadow of the Cross*
> *Though Christ be slain and Mary still a maid?*

Legends about the tree date from the days of Adam: one relates that Adam fell sick and sent his son Seth to the Garden of Eden to beg the angel guarding the gate for a little precious oil distilled from the tree of Life. The angel replied that it could not be obtained for 5,000 years, when the Son of God would visit the earth. As a consolation he gave him a little slip from the tree which Seth planted on Adam's grave. It grew and divided itself into three branches – cedar, cypress and olive. The tree and its descendants survived in the valley of Hebron through the days of Moses, David and Solomon, and was eventually used for making the Cross. The story has its variants such as the angel giving Seth three seeds which he places in Adam's mouth on his burial. Another legend suggests that David removed the miraculous tree to a fountain near Jerusalem where he composed his Psalms.

In plant lore cedar symbolizes beauty, constancy, health restorer, immortality, incorruptibility, majesty, mercy, pride, prosperity and strength. Cedar of Lebanon is the birthday emblem for 18 December with the sentiment of incorruptibility. The cedar cone is a life charm and the cedar leaf, in the language of the flowers means 'Think of me; I live only for you.' The medieval belief was that cedar wood was imperishable, but in the last century it was thought not to have 'answered its old reputation'. The botanist and horticulturalist Dr Lindley, hedging his bets slightly, called it the 'worthless though magnificent Cedar of Lebanon'. Nevertheless it was described recently in the *Field Guide to Shrubs and Trees* as 'dense, strong and extremely durable'. Cedar wood, being sweet-scented and a useful insect repellent, is also used to line clothes drawers.

CYPRESS

That cypress wrongly called of Monterey.
How wrongly I have seen
At Monterey where sand is silver-clean
And the Pacific azure to Cathay
And nothing passes but a passing ship,
That different tree upon its moon-white strand,
Twisted and dark, alone with sea and sand.
'The Garden' VITA SACKVILLE-WEST

CYPRESS (*Cupresses*). The generic name is derived from the Greek word *kuo* meaning I produce, and *parises,* meaning equal, in reference to the symmetrical growth of many of the species. The cypress was introduced to the Mediterranean regions by the Phoenicians, who came from Asia Minor and colonized the island of Cyprus, from which the tree derives its name. A more recent member of the family, *cupressocyparis ley-landii,* was introduced in 1888 as a cross between Monterey and Nootka cypresses. Their popularity as a fast-growing hedge, some would say barrier, is often the cause of considerable dissent. Like the yew, in earlier times cypress was planted in churchyards, often taking on the appearance of dark sentinels. In 'Giorno dei Morti' D.H. Lawrence wrote:

Along the avenue of cypresses,
All in scarlet cloaks and surplices
Of linen, go the chanting choristers,
The priests in gold and black, the villagers.

In both Greek and Roman mythology cypress was an emblem of the gods of the Underworld, the Fates and the Furies. In ancient Greece the tree was an attribute of Aphrodite and was carried in the annual processions in which she lamented over the death of Adonis. It was also sacred to Cyparissus, a youth loved by Apollo, who accidentally killed one of Apollo's favourite stags. This so preyed on his mind that he pined away and died. Apollo had the gods transform him into a cypress tree which then became the symbol of the immortal soul and eternal death. In Roman mythology cypress is dedicated to Dis, god of the infernal regions. Christopher Marlowe wrote:

> *Silvanus weeping for the lovely boy*
> *That is now turn'd into a cypress tree,*
> *Under whose shades the wood-gods love to be*

The tree from which Christ's cross was made was the cause of much speculation among earlier writers. The Venerable Bede (673–735) suggested four types of wood – cypress, cedar, pine and box – and this was generally accepted by contemporary monks. However, a translation of some Latin lines on the very subject suggests otherwise:

> *Nailed were his feet to Cedar, to Palm his hands,*
> *Cypress His body bore, title on Olive stands.*

In plant lore cypress is the birthday emblem for 11 February, signifying a just man. It is symbolic of death, despair, eternal sorrow, immortality, rebirth and mourning:

> *Frail as thy love, the flowers were dead*
> *Ere yet the evening sun was set:*
> *But years shall see the cypress spread,*
> *Immutable as my regret*

wrote Thomas Peacock in 'The Grave of Love'.

Formerly it was the custom to place cypress branches at the door of a house of the dead and it was also carried by the mourners in a funeral procession as a sign of irrevocable death – once cut, it will never grow. A short poem by Thomas Stanley, written in 1651, includes the yew:

Yet strew
Upon my dismal grave
Such offerings as you have,
Forsaken Cypresse, and sad Ewe

In a short extract from 'A Mayden's Song for her Dead Lover' we find this and other mourning customs:

Every hand, and every head
Bind with Cypresse, and sad Ewe,
Ribands black, and candles blue,
For him that was of men most true.

Mindful of the pitfalls of class distinction, William Coles, the author of *Adam in Eden*, reminded his readers that 'Cypresse garlands are of great account at funeralls amongst the gentiler sort, but Rosemary and Bayes are used by the commons both at funeralls and weddings. They are all plants which fade not a good while after they are gathered, and used to imitate unto us that the remembrance of the present solemnity might not dye presently, but be kept in mind for many yeares.'

And Cypress which doth Biers adorn,

is mentioned in *Poole's English Parnassus* (1657). The durable wood of the cypress is unlikely to be attacked by worms; the people of Athens used it for the coffins of their heroes and statues of their gods. The imperishable chests containing Egyptian mummies were also made of cypress wood.

Herbalists used the leaves, boiled in sweet wine or mead for healing wounds and to staunch the flow of blood. Mixed with barley meal they were used as a poultice for treating ulcers and carbuncles.

ELDER

Seek the bank where flowering elders crowd,
Where, scattered wide, the lily of the vale
Its balmy essence breathes, where cowslips hang
The dewy head, where purple violets lurk,
With all the lovely children of the shade.
'Spring' JAMES THOMSON

ELDER (*Sambucus nigra*). The generic name is probably connected with the Latin word *sambuca*, meaning harp, for which the wood was used. However, the name sambuke was applied to several musical instruments from the fact that they were all made of elder wood; for instance, *sackbutan* is an ancient Roman musical instrument. *Nigra* simply means black. The word elder comes from the Anglo-Saxon *aeld*, meaning fire, allegedly from the custom of blowing through the elder stem to revive dying embers – the pith pushes out very easily. The hollow pipe was a first step to making music – and also a pea shooter! Elder or eller was also called a bour or bore tree:

> *Bour tree – Bour tree: crooked rong*
> *Never straight and never strong;*
> *Ever bush and never tree*
> *Since our Lord was nailed to thee.*

The source of these lines is an old tradition claiming that the Cross of Calvary was made from the wood. A further common medieval belief suggests elder was the tree on which Judas Iscariot hung himself. In Langland's, 'Vision of Piers Plowman' it says:

> *Judas he japed with Jewen silver*
> *And sithen an eller hanged hymselve.*

As a consequence the tree became an emblem of sorrow and death and numerous superstitions sprang from the legends. The mushroom-like excrescences that grow on the elder are known as Judas (Jews') ears, and are said to have grown there since that time.

Elder has always had evil associations in folklore and legend with its connections with death and witchcraft. In England it was thought to be unlucky to bring the wood into the house as it would bring in the Devil; to burn the wood brought death to a member of the family. For the superstitious, cutting the tree down first required that deferential courtesies be extended to the elder-tree mother. Head bared, partly bended knee and folded arms, with the polite request 'Lady Ellhorn, give me some wood, and I will give thee some of mine when it grows in the forest' was most acceptable. The less respectful chose a more direct approach:

Owd girl, give me thy wood,
And I will give thee some of mine
When I grow into a tree.

If a tree was chopped down without permission the elder mother would cause the wood to creak or warp if it was made into furniture. Elder wood was never used for meat skewers or in shipbuilding. In *Art of Simpling* (1656) Coles stated that in the latter part of the seventeenth century 'in order to prevent witches from entering their houses, the common people used to gather Elder leaves on the last day of April and affix them to their doors and windows'. He added that the tree was cultivated near cottages for protection against lightning and witches. This in fact had a practical purpose because if the chosen site sheltered the house larder, it was said to deter flies. Green elder branches were also buried in graves or planted nearby, to protect the dead; in some parts of the country the driver of the hearse carried a whip of elder. The whole tree has a distinctive odour – some would say a ghastly smell – and sleeping under its shade was considered unwise as no plant will grow underneath. In plant lore it is the birthday flower for 29 March, and symbolizes compassion and zealousness. With all the superstitions and legends it is hard to believe that the elder, with its beautiful array of saucer-shaped cream blossoms in the spring and colourful autumn sprays of blue-black berries, which are ripe when they hang down in tassels, was once referred to as 'the medicine chest of the country people'. Pliny refers to its use as a medicine and so it has continued through the centuries with herbalists extolling its virtues; the more superstitious, however, thought these virtues were enhanced if it was found growing in the decayed stump of a hollow where a bird had dropped the seed!

The *Anatomie of the Elder*, translated from the Latin and published in 1644, was entirely devoted to its uses. Even Shakespeare makes reference to ancient medical authorities in *The Merry Wives of Windsor*:

> *What says my Aesculapius? My Galen? My heart of Elder?*

John Evelyn wrote of the tree: 'If the medicinal properties of its leaves, bark and berries

50

were fully known, I cannot tell what our countryman could ail for which he might not fetch a remedy from every hedge, either for sickness, or wounds.' The bark, leaves, flowers and berries all had a medicinal use.

Some of the many remedies included leaves boiled soft with a little linseed oil for piles and an infusion of the leaves to repel, and to soothe the skin after, insect bites. The young leaves and stalks were used for expelling phlegm and the bite of mad dogs, toothache and melancholy. An old remedy for a cough included a magical rhyme:

> *For a cough take Juda Eare*
> *With the paring of a Peare;*
> *And drinke this without feare;*
> *If you will have a remedie.*

Elderflower wines of today have their roots in a past when 'ale in which the Elder flowers have been infused is esteemed by many so salubrious that it is to be had in most of the eating houses about town.' In Kent entire orchards of elder trees were cultivated for making 'so called British wine.' It was said that 'judiciously flavoured with vinegar and sugar and small quantities of port wine, Elder is often the basis of spurious clarets and Bordeaux.' Although this lucrative practice was eventually banned there were those who claimed that the addition of elderberries cured their sciatica, neuralgia and rheumatism.

E LM

Huge elm, with rifted trunk all notched and scarred,
Like to a warrior's destiny! I love
To stretch me often on thy shadowed sward,
And hear the laugh of summer leaves above;
Or on thy buttressed roots to sit, and lean
In careless attitude, and there reflect
On times, and deeds, and darings that have been.
'Salters Tree' JOHN CLARE

English Elm (*Ulmus procera*). The generic name is the Latin word for the tree which gave it its Anglo-Saxon name, ulm or elm. There are several species of elm such as wych elm, smooth-leaved elm and Dutch elm. Although the English elm is thought to be a native tree it was only during the eighteenth and nineteenth centuries when it was planted along the hedgerows used to enclose farmland, that it achieved some prominence in the countryside.

The green elm with the one great bough of gold
Lets leaves into the grass slip, one by one

wrote Edward Thomas of the tree in his poem 'October'. Landscape gardeners too, mindful of its stately appearance and ability to retain its leaves into late autumn, increasingly used the elm in planning large gardens and parklands. Before the ravages of Dutch elm disease which entered the country in 1967 and resulted in the destruction of an estimated 25 million English elm, it was described as typical of the lowland English landscape. In 'Hawthorne' Henry Longfellow wrote:

And the great elms o'erhead
Dark shadows wove on their aerial looms
Shot through with golden thread.

In spring crimson flowers adorn the branches of the tree although it was the leaves that followed which were of interest to our ancestors, who, observing their size in spring had a guide to the sowing of various vegetables and crops:

> *When the elmen leaf is as big as a mouse's ear*
> *Then to sow barley never fear.*
> *When the elmen leaf is as big as an ox's eye,*
> *Then says I, 'Hie, boys! Hie!'*

A variation is:

> *When Elm leaves are as big as a shilling*
> *Plant kidney Beans, if to plant 'em your willing.*
> *When Elm leaves are as big as a penny,*
> *You must plant Kidney beans, if you mean to have any.*

In his poem 'The Dear Old Village', John Betjeman gives a delightful description of the foliage amidst the sound of church bells:

> *The elm leaves patter like a summer shower*
> *As lin-lan-lone pours through them from the tower*

However, if elm leaves were to fall out of season that was a bad omen – cattle would become diseased. According to Norse mythology, the whole human race sprang from the ash tree, from which man, Ask, was made, and the elm, from which the woman, Embla, was shaped.

In parts of England the maypole was traditionally an elm trunk which was brought home to the village, painted and decorated in preparation for the May Day festival. William Wordsworth wrote of the 'Joyful Elm,

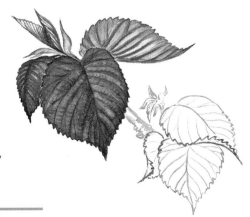

Around whose trunk the maidens dance in May'. Formerly elm branches were carried during the beating of the bounds ceremony on Rogation Days, the three days leading up to Ascension Day (the fortieth day after Easter) when the litany was sung in public places. They were also known as Gang Days. Children, accompanied by clergy and other local officials, walked their parish from end to end; the boys were lashed with willow wands on the boundary lines, a less than gentle reminder of the confines of the parish. A pole decorated with flowers, particularly milkwort, was carried by 'charity' children. Garlands of flowers were also used. Gerard wrote of the practice in Tudor times as the 'decking up of houses and banquetting-rooms, for places of pleasure, and for beautifying of streets in Crosse or Gang Week.' When the burning of a Yule log was a traditional event, a heavily grained green block of elm was chosen, for as long as the wood burnt the servants could drink the best and strongest cider. The ancient Greeks and Romans twined their vines round elm which they trained into convenient shapes and although vines were common in England during the sixteenth century reference to this practice is hard to find. The following authors may have just been following the classical writers, such as William Shakespeare in *A Comedy of Errors*:

> *Thou art an Elm, my husband, I a Vine,*
> *Whose weakness married to thy stronger state*
> *Makes me with thy strength to communicate.*

Or William Browne in his *Britannia Pastorals*:

> *She, whose inclination*
> *Bent all her courses to him-wards, let him know*
> *He was the Elm, whereby her vine did grow.*

Or John Milton:

> *They led the Vine*
> *To wed the Elm; she, spoused, about his twines*
> *Her marriageable arms, and with her brings*

Her dower, the adopted clusters to adorn
His barren leaves.

Even Edmund Spenser, who paid tribute to each tree in turn, referred to it as 'the vine-prop Elm'.

In plant lore elm signifies beauty, charm, courtesy, dignity, graciousness, shade and stateliness. A withered elm symbolizes adversity. The superstitious regarded a riding-switch cut from an elm tree as a lucky talisman. As the wood is close-grained, tough and knot-free, not liable to split or crack when seasoned and is remarkably durable under water, it was in demand in the days before cast-iron for water pipes, keels, bilge planks and harbour work. It was also used for coffins and consequently associated with the dead. Chaucer (1340–1400) speaks of it as 'the piler Elme, the cofre unto careyne' (carrion) in the *Parliament of Fowles*. The wood is ideal for furniture, particularly the seats of chairs but also the hubs of wooden wheels into which spokes have been driven. Elm boards were largely used for lining the interior of wagons, carts and wheelbarrows.

Herbalists used the dried inner bark of the tree. Culpepper, who designated elm a cold Saturnine plant, recommended the bruised leaves to heal wounds which should then be bound with elm bark. He also recommended the leaves or bark with vinegar for scurf and leprosy and with the addition of the roots for healing broken bones. Elm roots boiled for a long time in water 'the fat arising on the top thereof being clean skimmed off when applied where hair that had fallen away will quickly restore them.' The bark, ground with brine and pickled until it formed a poultice, and placed on the part pained with gout, was said to 'giveth great ease'. A decoction of the bark in water was alleged to be excellent 'for places as have been burnt with fire.' Under the title of Ulmus, it was officially registered in the *British Pharmacopoeia* of 1864.

FIELD MAPLE

'Green leaves, what are you doing
Up there on the tree so high?'
'We are shaking hands with the breeze
As they go singing by.'
'What, green leaves! Have you fingers?'
Then the Maple laughed with glee:
'Yes, just as many as you have;
Count us, and you will see!'
'The Five-Fingered Maple' KATE LOUISE BROWN

FIELD MAPLE (*Acer campestre*). The generic name is Latin for the tree, meaning sharp; the wood was used to make pointed weapons such as lances, pikes and spears. The bark of this low-growing hedgerow tree is deeply furrowed, which made the wood a popular commodity with Kentish farmers, who used it for poles in the hop fields – the rough surface giving warmth and purchase to the young hop vines. However, it is the beauty of the wood, when polished, which found favour with the Romans; Pliny records the wealthier members of society giving large sums of money for tables causing their wives, when accused of extravagance of dress and jewellery, to enquire about the cost of maple tables. The wood is compact, fine-grained and is often beautifully veined. Centuries ago it was commonly used for bowls and trenchers. John Milton (1608–74) wrote in 'Comus':

For who would rob a hermit of his weeds
His few books, or his beads, or maple dish,
Or do his grey hairs any violence?

Nevertheless, some of these bowls were ornately carved with inscriptions, others depicted scenes from legends with fine representations of animals, flowers and fruit. Edmund Spenser

describes an elaborate medieval drinking bowl known as a
'mazer'.

A mazery wought of the maple warre,
Wherein is encased many a fayre sight
Of bears and tygers, that maken fiers warre,
And ever tem spread a goodly wilde vine,
Entailed with a wanton yvy twine,
Thereby is a lambe in the wolve's jawes;
But see how fast runneth the shepherd swain,
To save the innocent from the beaste's pawes.

Saints too were a popular choice of subject. St Christopher, protector of sailors and ferrymen, was usually found carved in the bottom, in theory to comfort the drinker, as he drained his bowl.

According to the *Field Guide to Trees and Shrubs of Great Britain* the wood was used for violin making, the quality of the instrument owing much to the way that the wood was seasoned and to the composition of the finishing varnish. The wood formed the back, sides and neck of the instrument. Antonio Stradivari (1644–1737), the Italian violin maker of Cremona, who is estimated to have made a thousand musical instruments, was the first to use a bridge of maple to support the strings. The wood was also used for making harps, one such instrument being allegedly excavated from a Saxon barrow at Taplow in Berkshire, while another frame was part of the treasure recovered from the Sutton Hoo burial ship in Suffolk. Medieval carvers favoured the shape of the leaf, leaving this attractive design in many English churches, particularly on the pew ends. The beautiful veining in the wood and the knotted roots were also favoured by cabinet makers who used it for delicate inlay features, panelling and small objects. The distinctive pattern of 'bird's eye maple' is achieved by cutting across small knots in the trunk.

In plant lore maple is the birthday flower for 12 March, symbolic of conjugal love, earthly happiness, reserve, retirement. Its bright autumn colours typify past happiness, because it fades early and suggests transitoriness. A red or yellow leaf signifies the waning year.

The field maple is usually to be found in Southern England, growing in hedgerows and parks, sometimes to a considerable height. The dull green leaves of summer with their downy underside, slowly give way to the glorious show of its golden autumnal cloak – a memorable sight. Field maple can form an interesting hedge, when trimmed, and was, in the past, used for topiary. Herbalists recommended a concoction from the leaves and bark for the treatment of liver complaints. Superstitious people firmly believed that children passed through the branches of a tree would have a long life.

FIG

FIG (*ficus carica*). The succulent fruit of this tree has been valued, fresh or dried, from the earliest days. Indigenous to the Mediterranean regions it now grows wild in most of these countries. The Greeks are said to have received it from Caria in Asia Minor – hence its specific name – and it constituted one of their main sources of sustenance. It was used by the Spartans, noted for their frugal diet, at their public table. Athletes fed almost entirely on the fruit in the belief that it improved their strength and swiftness. Figs were such a valuable staple food to the ancient Greeks that a law was passed forbidding the exportation of those of a better quality. Following their introduction to Italy, Pliny recorded at least twenty-nine varieties, also stating that fresh figs formed a large part of the diet of slaves and agricultural workers. The fruit was most probably introduced to England by the Romans, although the tree may have come later. One account suggests that Cardinal Reginald Pole (1500–58) adviser to Queen Mary – planted the first tree at Lambeth Palace. Although fig trees have been cultivated for a long time in the South of England for their ornamental foliage – thick leathery leaves with three to five lobes – they can also be found flourishing in the most unlikely areas of the country, as Richard Mabey's recent *Flora Britannica* will testify. The fig was certainly familiar to the English dramatist Ben Jonson (1572–1637), as his poem 'To Penshurst' suggests:

The early Cherry, and Quince, with the later Plum,
Fig, Grape and Quince, each in his time doth come:
The blushing Apricot and woolly Peach
Hang on thy wals and every child may reach.
And though thy wals be of the country stone,
They'are rear'd with no man's ruine, no man's grone;
There's none, that dwell about them, wish them downe.

The fig that we eat is a combination of fruit and flower – a hollow fleshy receptacle enclosing numerous flowers, which never see the light, yet come to full perfection and ripen their seed. In Britain, even in ideal conditions – planted outside against a south-facing wall – the fruit does not generally ripen well or achieve the two crops a year, familiar in warmer climates (where one can savour the succulent richly-coloured flesh). The fruits are hard and green the first year, ripening in the second year. Nevertheless, growing freely, with its natural wide spread of branches from the decoratively pale grey, streaked trunk, the tree can attain heights of 26 feet – an unusual feature in any garden. Charles Dickens (1812–70) was obviously familiar with the tree; Captain Cuttle in *Dombey and Son* is advised to 'Train up a fig-tree in the way it should go, and when you are old sit under the shade of it.'

For some reason figs were closely associated with Palm Sunday and an old provincial name for the festival was Fig Sunday. Figs were eaten on that day in commemoration of the blasting of the barren fig tree by Jesus (Mark X 1), which took place on the day following the triumphant entry into Jerusalem. In many counties figs and fig pudding were eaten to celebrate the occasion. A mid-Lent speciality, fig or fag pie was also popular, consisting of short pastry, a half pound of figs, water, cornflour, mixed spice, a dessertspoonful of treacle and a few currants. Constance Cruikshank in *Lenten Fare and Food for Fridays*, records that in the nineteenth century crowds gathered to eat figs on the Dunstable Downs and on Silbury Hill in Wiltshire. Matthew Arnold (1822–88), the English poet and critic in 'The Scholar Gypsy' recalls the green fig, along with other delicacies being traded among the Aegean islands:

> . . . *saw the merry Grecian coaster come,*
> *Freighted with amber grapes, and Chian wine*
> *Green Bursting figs, and tunnies steeped in brine;*

In plant lore the fig tree is a symbol of the conjugal act, marriage, prolificacy, purgation and truth. It is called the tree of many breasts, inasmuch as its fruit, without any show of blossom, is visible before its leaves. Combining attributes that are both masculine (leaves) and feminine (fruit), it is held as symbolic of life and love. The Tree of Knowledge of Good and Evil is sometimes said to be a fig tree. In Sanscrit it is called Bo – the sacred tree of Buddhists. It is sacred to Dionysus, the Greek god of vegetation, who derived corpulency and strength from it. A fig tree symbolizes a holy life rich with fruits of the spirit. A fig leaf symbolizes the male principle. In Hebraic–Christian tradition, it symbolizes the fall from divine grace, immodesty, nakedness, shame; alluding to the fig leaf in art, depicting the first partial covering of Adam. In Victorian times, statues of naked men were fitted with tin fig leaves. The fruit is the birthday emblem of 10

July and in the language of the flowers it means: 'I keep my secret'. It symbolizes abundance, breasts, kisses, longevity, lust and the female principle. In ancient ceremonies of sacrifice, humans, before being put to death, were hung about with figs and scourged with the rod of the fig tree.

According to Ovid (43 BC–AD 17), among the celebrations of the first day of the year, Romans gave presents of figs and the inhabitants of Cyrene crowned themselves with fig wreaths when sacrificing to Saturn in the belief that he had discovered the fruit. The wolf that suckled Romulus and Remus is said to have rested under a fig tree.

In Europe during Shakespeare's time there was a grossly insulting gesture, made with an upturned thumb, called 'making a fig ' which he alludes to on several occasions, twice for instance in *Henry IV, Part II*:

> *When pistol lies, do this; and Fig me, like*
> *The bragging Spaniard*

and

> *Die and be damned, and Figo for thy friendship.*

In other quotations he simply likens the fruit to something of no importance as is 'Virtue! A Fig!' in *Othello*. However in *A Midsummer Night's Dream*, when the enchanted Titania bids the fairies to favour Bottom, it is simply another fruit:

> *Be kind and courteous to this gentleman,*
> *Hop in his walks and gamble in his eyes:*
> *Feed him with apricocks and dewberries,*
> *With purple grapes, green figs and mulberries.*

Cleopatra in *Anthony and Cleopatra* must have held the fruit in high esteem, when she declared 'O excellent! I love long life better than Figs'. In medieval times the fig was used to conceal poison, so that 'to fig a man' was a term for giving someone a fateful mouthful.

HAWTHORN

Among the many buds proclaiming May,
Decking the field in holiday array,
Striving who shall surpass in braverie,
Mark the faire blooming of the Hawthorn tree,
Who, finely cloathed in a robe of white,
Fills full the wanton eye with May's delight.
Britannia's Pastorals WILLIAM BROWNE

HAWTHORN (*Crataegus monogyna*). The generic name is from the Greek word *kratos* meaning strength, and alludes to the hardness of the wood. Hawthorn is a corruption of the Old English *hagathorn* or *haegthorn*, signifying a hedge – haw is also an old name for a hedge. It is also known as quickset or quickthorn as it grows as a quick or living hedge. It was used extensively during the land enclosures of the sixteenth to the eighteenth century, the remains of which can be seen today. Hawthorn hedges are particularly noticeable when they have escaped the distinctive layering crafts of earlier times and formed a boundary of small trees, which can attain heights of thirty feet. Hagthorn, haw, ladies' meat, bread and cheese, May blossom and perhaps the most popular, May, from the time it flowers, are all well-known names.

O thou merry month complete
May, thy very name is sweet!
May was maid in olden times,

And is still in Scottish rhymes;
May is the blooming hawthorn bough,
May's the month that's laughing now.

wrote the poet and essayist Leigh Hunt (1774–1859). Many country people thought that the blossoms, which transform the landscape in spring, carried the smell of the Great Plague. By autumn the spring berries are replaced by brilliant red berries, which are mealy but edible, and known as chucky cheese, pixie pears and cuckoo's beads, or as John Clare would say of them at Martinmas:

Crimsoned with awes the awthorns bend.

Hawthorn is best known for its association with May Day celebrations in earlier times. Bourne, in his *Antiquities,* tells us 'all ranks of people went a maying'. This was a happy occasion when branches of the blossom were gathered by young people while music and horn-blowing adding to the gaiety. They returned at sunrise to decorate their homes with a flowering branch over each doorway. May Day songs expressed the joy of the festival.

We have been rambling all the night,
And almost all the day,
And now returning back again,
We have brought you a bunch of May.

Innocent though the custom was in design it did degenerate into more decadent celebrations and church reformers eager to abolish May Day celebrations, with their pagan roots, gradually succeeded in doing so. Hawthorn was often the wreath of the Green Man or Jack-in-the-green, who, concealed in a wicker frame decorated with may branches, took part in the chimney sweeps' revels on May Day. In some parts of England those not wearing a sprig of hawthorn were doused in water. In ancient times the Floralia, dedicated to Flora, goddess of flowers and spring – said to give sweetness to honey, fragrance to blossom, aroma to wine and charm to youth – was portrayed as a young woman garlanded with flowers. Her festival was celebrated with mimes, games and 'much licence' from 28 April to 1 May and reflected the crowning of the May Queen of more recent times. The dew from the hawthorn, especially on May Day, was said to make plain girls beautiful.

The fair maid who the first of May,
Goes to the field at the break of day,
And washes in dew from the Hawthorn tree
Will ever after handsome be.

Hawthorn was used as a love oracle on May Eve. A girl would hang a branch from a signpost and her future husband would come from the direction that it pointed in the morning Should it fall to the ground there would be no wedding. A safer alternative was in the belief that a girl should partly break the first branch of hawthorn she saw, but leave it hanging. That night she would dream of her future husband; she should return in the morning to pick the branch. Superstitions surrounding the hawthorn vary from county to county but one common to all was that death was alleged to follow when may blossom was taken indoors. Even sitting under a hawthorn tree in May had its dangers – fairies would mysteriously gain power over you. For those keen to seek protection from such spirits, witches and storms, a bunch of hawthorn gathered on Palm Sunday or Ascension Day, by someone unconnected with the home, and placed in the rafters, ensured complete safety. For those not wishing to court disaster the protective virtues of the hawthorn against injury in a storm can be found in the old rhyme:

Beware of an oak,
It draws the stroke,
Avoid an ash,
It courts a flash,
Creep under the thorn,
It will save you from harm.

In the Christian tradition it is a holy tree associated with the Virgin Mary. In Christian legend there is much speculation as to whether it is the alleged Glastonbury Thorn of Somerset which early Christians associated with Joseph of Arimathea who came to England to preach the Gospel. According to legend, having arrived at the Isle of Avalon he thrust his staff into the ground and slept. On waking he found it had been transformed into a tree with snowy white blossom. Taking this as a sign he built a chapel which later became a magnificent abbey. The tree was said to produce flower buds on Christmas Eve that bloomed on Christmas Day and withered away the following night. News of this remarkable tree quickly spread and people collected the blossoms and pieces of thorn.

Historically, the hawthorn was used as a crest by the Tudors. After the Battle of Bosworth, which ended the Wars of the Roses, the symbolic crown of the defeated Richard III was found hanging in a hawthorn bush. An old proverb refers to the incident 'Cleave to the crown though it hang in a bush.'

In plant lore hawthorn bears the sentiment of contentment. It is symbolic of fertility, marriage, hope, fruitfulness, self-denial and spring. In Greek mythology, the hawthorn lighted the temples of Hymen, the god of marriage, and the flowers were used in bridal wreaths

Hawthorn timber was used to make small articles – the fine grained wood acquires a beautiful polish – and the root-wood for making boxes and combs. As a fuel it is said to produce the best heat. The leaf buds were known as 'bread and cheese' and were eaten between slices of bread and butter. Both flowers and berries are astringent for sore throats. The haws bruised and boiled in wine were recommended by herbalisst, without specifying the amount to be drunk, for easing pains. A good liqueur is made from hawthorn berries infused in brandy. When tea was an expensive commodity the dried hawthorn leaves were added, and passed off as real tea.

HAZEL

Small beauty hath my unsung flower,
For spring to own, or summer hail;
But, in the season's saddest hour,
To skies that weep and winds that wail,
Its glad surprisals never fail.
'Hazel Blossoms' JOHN GREENLEAF WHITTIER

HAZEL (*Corylus avellana*). The generic name is the Greek word for hazel. Hazel is derived from the Old English *hael* or *haesel*. The tree, with its conspicuous oval sawtooth-edged oval leaves, is common throughout Britain. Hazel produces male flowers, once known as *agglettes* or *blowinges,* now as 'lambstail' catkins and female flowers, tiny buds with red tassels, which appear simultaneously in February. Hazel produces the symbols of beauty and wisdom at the same time, hence it was known as the tree of poetic art. The edible nuts grow in clusters each partially covered in leafy bracts.

This long-established tree has been successfully farmed for hundreds of years by coppicing – a method whereby large bushes are cut back to ground level about every seven years – and supplied the building trade with panels of interwoven hazel rods, known as wattles, which when secured between wooden frames (generally made of oak) were treated with a mixture of straw and mud. This method of construction was known as wattle and daub, examples of which can still be seen today. The tradition of using untreated wattle for fencing and enclosures is still part of our heritage. The pliant hazel rods were used

in basket work and also hedge-laying when they were inter-twined with a partially diagonally cut and layered hedge. This dying craft, known as 'plashing', needed great expertise to bring about a most attractive but practical result. A Y-shaped hazel branch is still used for water divining – the diverging arms are held firmly in the hands with the shaft pointing forward:

> *And as within the hazel's bough*
> *A gift of mystic virtue dwells,*
> *That points to golden ores below,*
> *And in dry desert places tells*
> *Where flow unseen the cool, sweet wells.*

Superstition decreed that a divining rod should be cut when facing east so that the branch caught the first rays of the morning sun, or, as some say, the eastern and western sun must shine through the fork of the rod or it will be good for nothing.

> *Some sorcerers do boast they have a rod,*
> *Gather'd with vowes and sacrifice,*
> *And (bourne about) will strangely nod*
> *To hidden treasure where it lies.*

Many superstitions surround the tree. A breastband of hazel was fastened onto the harness of a horse to protect it against evil spirits. In Ireland cattle were driven through blazing fires on Midsummer Night and had their backs singed with hazel rods, which were then saved for cattle droving during the following year. Despite the fact that a twig of hazel was said to confer invisibility on the wearer, sea captains wore one in their hat as protection against bad weather. In medieval times the hazel rod served in courts of justice for discovering murderers and thieves. A hazel wand was carried by heralds as a badge of office and, in heraldry, along with barberry and dogberry, it was the device of the clan Colquhoun. The wands appear to have had religious associations too, possibly as a token of certain pilgrimages, as remains of hazel staves have apparently been found in graves of the clergy.

The Celts associated the tree with fire and fertility and placed small twigs in their homes as protection against lightning. Torches of burning branches of hazel were carried by the Romans at their Wedding Eve ceremonies to ensure a peaceful and happy union. In Norse mythology hazel is assigned to Thor, god of war.

Gathering hazel nuts in autumn – 'going a nutting' – was a jolly occasion. The nuts had to be very ripe, almost falling out of their cases, but stored in them in order to retain their moisture. Old books describe how the nutmeg nestles within its mace 'as the hazel in its green case'.

A children's rhyme suggests:

Fresh October brings the pheasant,
Then to gather nuts is pleasant.

However, an ancient custom, considered unlucky to miss, suggests an earlier month (Nutting or Holy Rood Day, 14 September). According to an old saying a good crop was a sinister omen: 'Many nuts, many pits.' Pit means a grave here. Hazelnuts were particularly associated with Hallowe'en, which was also known in some parts of England as Nutcrack Night. Fortune telling was the favourite amusement and the nuts were used in love divination rituals.

Two hazel nuts I threw into the flame,
And to each nut I gave a sweetheart's name:
This with the loudest bouncee me sore amaz'd
That in the flame of bright colour blaz'd,
As blaz'd the nut, so may thy passion grow
For 'twas thy Nut that did so brightly glow!

A briefer alternative was to name a nut after each girl present and as each nut was thrown into the fire, a name would be called in the belief that:

If you love me, pop and fly,
If not, lie and die.

On Nutting Day bonfires were lit and grain scattered for the wild birds to bring good luck to the farm. For those who dared wait in a church porch at midnight, the spirits of parishioners who would die during the coming year appeared.

The superstitious were reassured by various old wives' tales that prevention was better than cure – a double hazelnut carried in the pocket prevented toothache whilst another charm, traditionally used for curing the bite of an adder, required pieces of hazel, arranged in the form of a cross, to be laid on the wound, whilst a lengthy, baffling incantation was intoned:

> *Underneath this hazel din mote*
> *There's a maggoty worm with a speckled throat.*
> *Nine double is he;*
> *Now from nine double to eight double,*
> *And from eight double to seven double,*
> *And from seven double to six double …*
> *And from one double to no double,*
> *No double hath he.*

Roasted kernels sprinkled with pepper were recommended to be eaten before going to bed as a treatment for colds. The kernels also provided the basis for a mixture to treat lung complaints. The hazel is assigned to the planet Mercury and symbolizes justice, reconciliation and truth. In the language of the flowers it means 'Be wise and desist.' It was given by a girl to a boy as a sign of discouragement after unwanted attention.

HOLLY

Adventurous Holly! Through long summer days,
When fragile blossoms, following easier ways,
Joined in array of loveliness and bloom,
You seemed to guess that quickly to the tomb
They all must go; and you did wait, my dear,
Until the winter silence crowned the year.
'Holly' JOHN M. STUART-YOUNG

HOLLY (*Ilex aquifolium*). Holly or holm is from the Old English *holen* or *holegn*, a word derived from the Latin *ulex*, which in the Middle Ages was confused with *Ilex*, the holm oak of the ancients. Aquifolium means needle-leaved in Latin. The holly was formerly known as holme, hulver or hulfere, a name familiar to Geoffrey Chaucer:

> *Betwixt an Hulfere and a woodbende,*
> *As I was ware, I saw where lay a man.*

There are many cultivated varieties of this native hardy evergreen, with varying shapes, leaf colour and berries. Holly makes an impregnable hedge or an impressive ornamental shrub or tree where the leaves, on the higher branches, are often without the conspicuous sharp spines, as Robert Southey describes in 'Holly Tree':

> *Below a circled fence its leaves are seen*
> *Wrinkled and keen,*
> *No grazing cattle through their prickly round*
> *Can reach to wound;*
> *But as they grow where nothing is to fear,*
> *Smooth and unharmed their pointless leaves appear.*

In plant lore holly is the birthday flower for 5 March and is symbolic of domestic happiness, foresight, friendship and good wishes. In the language of the flowers it means: 'Am I forgotten?' In the Christian tradition it typifies suffering, the Passion of Christ; with the red berries, representing drops of blood, it typifies love unto death. An old rhyme suggests this association:

The holly bears a berry red,
The ivy bears a black 'un,
To show that Christ His blood did shed,
To save our souls from Satan.

The holly is also an attribute of St John. In ancient times holly was Saturn's club, the evergreen ruling the waning part of the year, and given as an emblem of goodwill. Boughs of holly were included with gifts at weddings and the festival of Saturn, the Saturnalia, celebrated on 17–19 December. This custom was later adopted by the early Christians, despite an edict from the authorities forbidding them to decorate their homes at this time. Eventually these so-called pagan customs became intertwined with the Christian faith and the origins were eventually

laid to rest. An old legend tells of holly springing up under the footsteps of Christ when he trod the earth. The spiky leaves and scarlet berries, like drops of blood, were thought to be symbolic of the saviour's suffering, and for this reason it was called Christ's Thorn. Holly and ivy were used in fertility rites during the earlier Fire Festivals (Christmas), the prickly variety representing the male principle and the entwining ivy the female principle. However, it is now regarded as a symbol of eternal life. Along with other evergreens, holly was hung in churches as a sign of welcome to elves and fairies. Today every church is decorated with floral offerings and the festival of Christmas is incomplete without a variety of beautiful greenery. In old church calendars Christmas Eve was marked *templa exornantor* (churches are decked). Many old carols allude to the holly:

> *Christmastide*
> *Comes in like a bride,*
> *With Holly and Ivy clad.*

Of course, the most familiar is 'The Holly and the Ivy.' Traditionally the holly must be hung before mistletoe in the home otherwise ill luck will come down the chimney on Christmas Eve – always considered a vulnerable point of entry for witches and evil spirits. After the Christmas festivities, holly must be taken down no later than Epiphany Eve (5 January) although older traditions say Candlemas (2 February).

A tree growing near the house was believed to protect the occupants against lightning and thunder – the dark green leaves and red berries, inside or outside a house, provided extra protection from demons, witches and the Evil Eye. Holly branches should never be burnt green, otherwise death will visit the family. To tread on a holly berry or bring a spray of the creamy white flowers into the house is also unlucky. Many berries foretell a hard winter. The superstitious thought that the male or prickly holly is lucky to men, and the smooth or variegated type, 'she-holly', to women. Naturally this difference was the basis of a love divination ceremony to induce dreams of a future husband or wife. Nine variegated holly leaves gathered on a Friday at midnight, were placed in a three-cornered handkerchief, tied with nine knots, and concealed under the pillow before going to bed. Absolute silence had to be maintained from picking the leaves until dawn.

Herbalists recommended an infusion of holly leaves be given for catarrh, pleurisy, fevers, rheumatism and smallpox. The juice of fresh leaves was 'employed with advantage in jaundice'. The berries, which are violently emetic, were sometimes used for treating dropsy, and also in a powder as an astringent to check bleeding. Culpepper wrote that 'The bark and leaves are good used as fomentations for broken bones and such members as are out of joint.' Stripped from the young shoots and allowed to ferment, the bark was the basis of birdlime, a sticky substance that was smeared onto branches to catch songbirds. It was also exported, to be used for destroying insects. Holly wood is hard and compact and beautifully white. It was used as a substitute for ebony on teapots, for mathematical instruments, for wood engraving, for the stocks of light driving whips and for walking sticks. It was much prized for ornamental work, being used extensively for inlays, such as on Tunbridge ware.

HORSE CHESTNUT

O chestnut-tree, great rooted blossomer,
Are you the leaf, the blossom or the bole?
O body swayed to music, O brightening glance,
How can we know the dancer from the dance.
'Among School Children' W. B. YEATS

HORSE CHESTNUT (*Aesculus hippocastanum*). The generic name is from the Greek, *esca,* meaning nourishment. The specific name is a translation of the common name which was given, according to John Evelyn, 'from it curing horses broken winded and other cattle of coughs'. For those who believe in sympathetic magic there is a 'sign' on the tree when the leaves fall from the branch – a horseshoe-shaped scar with small nail marks on the branch.

This large ornamental tree is a relative newcomer to the British landscape, having been introduced from the Balkans in the late sixteenth century. It was first raised in Northern Europe by the botanist Charles de l'Ecluse in 1576, from seeds brought from Constantinople. John Gerard described the tree in his *Herball* of 1597 with great accuracy although it is extremely unlikely that he had actually seen one at that time. 'The Horse Chestnut groweth ... to be a very great tree, spreading his great and large armes or branches far abroad, by which meanes it maketh a very coole shadow. These branches are garnished with many beautiful leaves, cut or divided into five, six or seven sections or divisions, like Cinkfoile, or rather like the leaves of Ricinus (castor-oil plant), but bigger. The flowers growe at the top of the stalkes, consisting of fewer small leaves like the Cherrie blossom, which turne into round, rough and prickley heads.'

Landscape gardeners were responsible for the majority of early plantings, which they undertook with great enthusiasm.

The ideal location for the horse chestnut was thought to be the grounds of large houses.

> *Oh! There the chestnuts, summer through,*
> *Beside the river make for you*
> *A tunnel of green gloom,*
> *And sleep deeply above*

wrote Rupert Brooke. Lancelot (Capability) Brown (1716–83), who acquired his name from telling his clients that their garden had excellent 'capabilities', is believed to have arranged the planting of 4,800 of the trees in the Tottenham Park estate in Wiltshire. Using this natural effect he laid out gardens, including those at Blenheim, Kew, Stowe and Warwick Castle. However, it was the architect Sir Christopher Wren, who was responsible in 1699 for the amazing mile-long Chestnut Avenue at Bushy Park north of Hampton Court, which was originally intended as a carriage drive for William III, to take him from Teddington to the palace. In 1838 Queen Victoria opened Hampton Court to the public and Bushy Park soon became a popular place for picnics, particularly when the trees were displaying their giant nosegays.

Chestnut Sunday was established in mid-May, and London Transport even advertised the occasion with scenic posters. According to Richard Mabey in *Flora Britannica*, one participant was so deeply impressed that he wrote of one such occasion: 'the sight is certainly remarkable and well worth seeing – a wide mile of lofty walls of foliage, bespangled with countless white spires – like tapering candles – and the boughs laden and almost sweeping the ground.' This

delightful custom had almost ceased by the 1920s and had died out by the Second World War. However, it was revived again for Queen Elizabeth's Jubilee in 1977. Chestnut Sunday is now celebrated on the nearest Sunday to 11 May. Those that join the party, which gathers at Teddington Gate at 12.30pm, supposedly comment on arrival at the meeting place, 'The candles are alight' and then walk down the avenue to the Diana Fountain where a picnic is held. By the beginning of the nineteenth century the horse chestnut could be seen in public parks, suburban streets and on village greens. However, it is in autumn when the green spiky fruit assumes a seasonal hue and cracks open to reveal a shiny mahogany coloured nut that the tree assumes a different role.

> *Calm in the morn without a sound,*
> *Calm as to suit a calmer grief,*
> *And only thro' the faded leaf*
> *The chestnut pottering to the ground*

wrote Tennyson. Children and adults collect these treasures as they fall from the tree and only then can the enjoyable pastime of 'playing conkers' begin. As the earlier trees were planted on private land the game itself is of comparatively recent origin. A similar game, using cobnuts, is recorded in the seventeenth century. Nuts were strung 'like the beads of a rosary', and the participants exchanged strikes with an opponent. There are various rules, rituals and rhymes associated with playing conkers, such as the rhyme:

> *Hobley, hobley, ack,*
> *Obbly obbly onker,*
> *My first conker*

which should be said at the start. The game involves two opponents, each with a 'conker' on a string, who take alternate strikes at the other's nut until one is completely broken. The winning 'conker' becomes a 'oner'. If, for instance, it then breaks a 'fiver', it absorbs the other's score and becomes a 'sixer'. Since 1965 a World Conker Championship has been

held in the village of Ashton in Northamptonshire on the second Sunday in October. The championship is said to have originated when a few friends who were unable to coarse fish because of bad weather amused themselves by playing conkers. They were not short of supplies because in the village there is a mile long horse-chestnut avenue up to the mansion and a fully grown tree has now been transplanted to shelter the new smithy. This may prove to be a useful asset as the tree was believed to deter gnats. An interesting connection can be made with a less harmless eighteenth century game played with snail shells – often occupied. The shells were pressed against one another and the survivor was 'the Conqueror'.

In plant lore horse chestnut is the birthday flower for 1 October and symbolizes luxury; because of the spiky burr surrounding the nut it typifies darting, piercing, radiating fire. The herbalist Culpepper assigned the tree to the planet Jupiter, advising 'the fruit must promote the good blood, and yield good nourishment to the body' although too many would cause headaches and constipation. The bark is said to have tonic, narcotic and febrifuge properties and an infusion was used to treat fevers and as an external application for ulcers. The fruit was recommended for rectal problems, neuralgia and rheumatism; begged or stolen it was believed to be a charm against the latter. In some countries the nut was once used for feeding cattle and horses, after first being soaked in lime water (in order to remove the bitter flavour) and then ground to a meal. In England experiments to prove their value as animal feed required the crushed nuts to be soaked overnight, then boiled for half an hour, drained, and dried, and then partially husked and ground.

JUNIPER

A few belated cloudberries linger on
High on the moist hill-breast where mists distil;
And now the prickly juniper displays
On dry warm banks his pungent fruitage blue.
'Autumn in the Highlands' J. C. SHAIRP

JUNIPER (*Juniperus communis*). The generic name is Latin
for this tree. The common juniper, one of Britain's native
conifers, may be a small conical tree or a twisted shrub with
spreading branches. It is quite often seen on moorlands, in the
Lake District and Scotland. John Whittier, in 'Last Walk of
Autumn' recalls the juniper in colourful seasonal company:

And on the ground of sombre fir,
And azure-studded juniper
The silver birch its buds of purple shows,
And scarlet berries tell where bloomed the sweet wild-rose.

Juniper berries ripen to dark purple
in their second year; consequently
blue and green fruit appear on
the same branch. They were collected in sacks and dried out on
shelves during which time
they would lose some of
their blue bloom and become
the more familiar black. The
volatile oil is the prime ingredient in Geneva or Holland's Gin.
The word gin is derived from the
French for juniper, *genievre*. In
warmer countries the tree yields, by

incision, a gum or varnish. The ancients believed that pungent smoke produced by burning the green branches was incense to the infernal gods. In the Middle Ages it was supposed that no witch would enter a house where there was a juniper bough over the door; anyone with an evil intent had to stop and count its leaves – an almost impossible task – and so intruders invariably left in despair. It was believed that the odour kept evil spirits at bay and smoked out witches. Bishop Hall (1764–1831) alludes to this notion in his 'Satires':

> *And with glasse stills, and sticks of Juniper,*
> *Raise the black spirit that burns not with fire.*

The berries were burnt at funerals to frighten away evil spirits. Nevertheless the scent of the tree made the spiky green needles much sought after as a strewing herb. Strewing was a delightful custom whereby sweet smelling leaves, herbs and flowers were scattered on the wooden or straw-strewn floors of houses and churches, primarily to alleviate the smells resulting from what could be described as less than pleasant habits of the time. For a similar reason juniper was also burnt in order to fumigate the bedchambers. Queen Elizabeth I is alleged to have favoured this particular herb. As the wood is aromatic, spits for roasting meat, and spoons were made from it in the belief that it imparted a pleasant flavour to the food. Until the end of the last century juniper boughs were cut for firewood – they gave off a distinctive fragrance. They were also used in the north of England as a base for haystacks.

The superstitious believed that chopping down a juniper tree would bring death to the family – probably one's own! Dreaming of the juniper tree was also unlucky though, strangely, to dream about juniper berries on their own was not.

In plant lore it is the birthday flower for 3 October and is symbolic of fecundity, longevity, succour, remembrance and protection. In the Old Testament it is referred to as a ministering spirit, and in Christian legend, the Virgin Mary took refuge, with the child Jesus, behind a juniper bush when fleeing from King Herod into Eygpt.

Through the centuries juniper berries were prescribed for all manner of ailments, from leprosy to fumigating the head and nightcap, so that one wonders how any household managed without it. Many learned men advised on its beneficial qualities, including Henry VIII's physician Andrew Borde, who used it 'for the infirmities of the ars and the fundement', first advising one 'to kepe the ars and buttockes warme. And syt not on cold erth, nor upon stone or stones.' The seat of the complaint was washed with a solution of juniper and water – 'after that make a perfume of Juneper and syt over it.' Culpepper praised it, saying 'this admirable solar shrub is scarce to be paralleled for its virtues.' He considered the berries to be effective against poison, the biting of venomous 'beasts' and also urinary complaints. He also advised that 'it is so powerful a remedy against the dropsy, that the very lye made of ashes of the herb being drunk, cures the disease … and expels wind; indeed there is scarce a better remedy for wind in any part of the body, or the colic, than the chemical oil drawn from the berries.' As an alternative, for those country people unable to extract the oil he suggested they 'may content themselves by eating a ten or a dozen ripe berries every morning fasting.' Physicians were later to recommend this treatment for lung complaints. Perhaps the most disgusting remedy comes from a recipe book of 1746, for vertigo or convulsions, which consisted of one ounce of juniper berries, two ounces of fresh Seville orange peel, three ounces of male piony root, three ounces of peacock's dung, eight ounces of sugar candy, infused in two quarts of wine for twenty-four hours in hot ashes then allowed to settle. 'Take two spoonsfulls of this in a glass of Angelica-water. It has done great cures.' Oil of Juniper has an ancient reputation as an abortifacient. In parts of Scotland the expression giving birth 'under the savin tree' suggested such a remedy had been used to procure a miscarriage. Juniper pills were advertised as 'The Lady's Friend' in women's magazines until quite recently. Juniper was prescribed in this century for urinary complaints, piles and worms, and the ash from burnt juniper wood as a remedy for gum complaints. Last but far from least, an infusion

of juniper was said to solve the eternal quest – restore lost youth. However, the recipe is not recorded. An unspecified juniper, known as 'the savage tree' was given in small quantities to horses in their feed 'to ginger them up'. One feels slightly mollified on discovering that *Flora Britannica* suggests that this could have been a cultivated variety, *juniper sabina*, known as 'savin' which yields the more potent and tonic oil of savarin. Today the berries are back in fashion as a culinary ingredient for game and venison dishes.

LARCH

Above our lane two rows of larches lean,
And lissom, rosy pines with wild black hair
One slim, bright fingered chestnut in between,
In blossom time and berry-time and snow
Are muffled sounds of feet that come and go
Forever, from the cones and falling spines.
'Humble Folk' MARY WEBB

LARCH (*Pinus larix*). *Larix* was the name given to pine resin by the ancient Greek physicians, and the term has been kept for these elegant trees. The tree was introduced at a date prior to 1629, from the mountainous regions of central Europe. It was first cultivated as an ornamental garden tree and much later for timber. The Dukes of Atholl, of Perthshire in Scotland, were promoters in this field during the mid-eighteenth century, planting, reputedly, eighteen million trees. The larch is a natural tree of the mountains, attaining greater heights and development in its wood in countries where the winters are longer and colder.

I have looked on the hills in the stormy North
And the larch has hung his tassels forth.
The fisher is out on the sunny sea,
And the reindeer bound o'er the pastures free

wrote Felicia Hemans in 'The Spring'. As a testimony to the late beauty of winter and early spring one only has to see the larch with its fresh green needle-shaped leaves and delicate red female flowers splashing the gaunt, sweeping folds of its branches, which already display the small dark cones of the previous year.

Alfred, Lord Tennyson wrote in 'In Memoriam':

When rosy plumelets tuft the larch,
And rarely pipes the mounted thrush
Or underneath the barren bush
Flits by the sea-blue bird of March

Larches are peculiar among conifers in that they are deciduous, scattering their yellow-orange coloured needles in the autumn, not, however, before they have delighted the eye with their colourful farewell from amongst their darker green companions of the conifer woods. In plant lore larch is the birthday flower for 26 October and is a symbol of audacity, boldness, impregnability, independence and stability. According to the *Flora Britannica*, one of the most remarkable trees in Suffolk is the 'Creeping Larch' of Henham Hall, which was planted in around 1800, and is the only one of its vintage. It stands in the pleasure grounds of the now demolished hall and while it is only 2.7 metres in height with a girth of less than 3 metres, the crown spreads for 26 metres north to south, and for 13 metres east to west. All of this reclines on a raised platform constructed from the railway tracks of the redundant Southwold line. In the past, it was the durability of the wood and its rapid growth which made it popular at a time of great expansion in the mining industry. It was also used in the sprawling railway system, for sleepers. Larch was also in demand for ship and house building and in cabinet work. Gilding was said to be more effective on its wood than any other type. Larch was also fastened behind pictures as it resisted attack from woodworm. The

rapid growth of the larch added to its value and, like the birch, it was used as a nursery tree for slow-growing and less hardy kinds of tree. Turpentine was collected from the full grown trees from May to October – holes were bored in the trunk, wooden tubes inserted and the liquid strained through a coarse hair-cloth to remove the impurities. This was used in varnish, commercially known as Venice Turpentine. Medicinally it was used as an external application in the treatment of chronic eczema and psoriasis. It was also recommended as a stimulant expectorant in chronic bronchitis and given internally for haemorrhaging and cystitis. When burnt the trees exude a gum which is soluble in water, similar to gum arabic, which was used for sticking paper and stiffening linen.

LEMON

Lemon (*Citrus limonia*). The generic name is the Latin word for another plant, but was applied by Linnaeus (1707–78) – Swedish naturalist and physician, founder of modern scientific nomenclature for plants and animals – to this genus, which also includes grapefruits, limes and oranges. The lemon, which is an evergreen, produces delicate, fragrant flowers, coloured white on the inside and tinged with pink on the outside. This small straggling tree was first introduced in 1595 and is a variety of citron first known to Europeans as the Median apple – having been brought from Media, an ancient region south-west of the Caspian sea. A Classics scholar aptly described the flavour:

Nor be the citron, Media's boast unsung
Though harsh the juice and lingering on the tongue.

The trees reached Europe through Persia or Media, although they were first grown in Greece and then in Italy, in 2AD. In England most lemon cultivars produce seeded fruit that may remain green rather than turning yellow. For successful growth in the open they require a temperature of 68 degrees. This well-known bright yellow fruit is an ovoid berry about three inches in length, and nipple-shaped at one end. At least fifty varieties have been developed over the centuries. In earlier times the importers ensured that the finer fruits from such places as Messina and Murcia arrived boxed and wrapped separately in paper. It was thought that lemons could be kept fresh for months if dipped in melted paraffin or varnished with shellac dissolved in alcohol. Inferior fruit was preserved in salt water and packed in barrels or as lemon juice. It is probably the most valuable fruit for preserving health and certainly the best of all antiscorbutics used to treat and prevent scurvy. Consequently, English sailing ships were required by law to carry sufficient lemon or lime juice for every seaman to have an ounce daily after being ten days at sea. The juice formed the basis of cooling drinks to allay thirst and fevers. Lemonade became a popular, even fashionable drink. Poets mentioned this new 'mineral', for example, Thomas Moore in *Intercepted Letters*:

> *A Persian's heaven is eas'ly made:*
> *'Tis but black eyes and lemonade.*

And John Betjeman in 'An Archaeological Picnic' gave encouragement to a member of the party with the words: 'Drink Mary, drink your fizzy lemonade!' Also C. S. Calverley (1831–84) in 'The Palace' sang of the still variety:

> *Such are the sylvan scenes that thrill*
> *This heart! The lawns, the happy shade,*
> *Where matrons, whom the sunbeams grill,*
> *Stir with slow spoon their lemonade.*

Slices of lemon and the rind gave an aromatic addition to tonics. Expression or distillation can obtain fragrant oil; however, methods vary in different countries. According to Mrs Grieve in *A Modern Herbal* (1931), in France 'Essence de Citron distilée' could be prepared simply by rubbing fresh lemons on a coarse tin grater and distilling the grated peel in water. The superior 'Essence de Citron au zeste' was a more elaborate procedure requiring a saucer-shaped pewter dish with a lip for pouring at one side, and a funnel sunk from the middle. In the bottom were sharp brass pins upon which the peel was rubbed. Peel was often pickled in brine and sold to manufacturers for candying. Candied peel was prepared by boiling the peel in syrup, then exposing it to the air until the sugar crystallized. Cookery books reveal that for centuries lemons have been widely used as flavouring in sauces, puddings, cakes and confectionery. William Shakespeare mentions the fruit in *Love's Labours Lost* in connection with a spice: 'A Lemon – Stuck with Cloves'.

Medicinally the juice, a good astringent, was recommended as a gargle for sore throats, uterine haemorrhaging after childbirth, pruritis of the scrotum and as a sunburn lotion. It was said to be the best cure for hiccups, hysterical palpitations of the heart and jaundice. A general remedy for scabs and itches was to sprinkle powder of brimstone on half a lemon, roast it and then rub it into the affected area. Apparently it was an excellent remedy for crab lice too.

In plant lore the lemon is the birthday emblem of 11 January, symbolic of discretion, pleasant thoughts and zest. It is sometimes depicted as the fruit of the Tree of Knowledge of Good and Evil. Lemon blossom is the birthday flower of 12 January, symbolizing fidelity.

In the English language, a lemon signifies a gullible person ñ one from whom anything is readily obtained – in allusion to squeezing the juice from the fruit. However Oliver Goldsmith (1728–74) in *She Stoops to Conquer*, uses it in reference to the passing of time: 'I'll be with you in the squeezing of the lemon'. While Sydney Smith (1771–1845) in *Lady Holland's Memoir* has her complaining: 'My living in Yorkshire was so far out of the way, that it was actually twelve miles from a lemon.' An unpleasant or worthless person is said to be a lemon and to be cheated is to be 'handed a lemon'.

LIME

And air swept lindens yield
Their scent, and rustle down their perfum'd showers
Of bloom on the bent grass where I am laid,
And bower me from the August sun with shade.
'The Scholar Gypsy' MATTHEW ARNOLD

COMMON LIME (*Tilia Xeuropaea*). The generic name is the one used by the Romans. The word lime is derived from the Anglo-Saxon *lind*, which became *lynde*, then *line*, hence its alternative name, linden. It means shield, as the wood, which is easy to handle, was used for that purpose. Being light and fine-grained it was also very popular for making musical instruments and for wood carving since at least the Middle Ages. Much of the exquisite work of the master craftsman Grinling Gibbons (1648–1720) was carried out in lime. Swags and garlands of flowers and fruit recently restored after the fire at Hampton Court by expert carvers have refocused attention on his work which can also be seen in larger country houses. Lime coppice was used in the same way as other woods for fuel and poles. As it does not splinter it is still used by morris men for 'thwacking' their partners' sticks during their energetic dance routines.

The common lime is the tallest broad-leaved tree in Britain and is thought to be a hybrid between the large-leaved and small-leaved limes. It can live for 500 years. In Roman times it was planted for its shade and sweet scented flowers – a favourite haunt of bees. Due to its rapid growth and fragrance, avenues of lime were popular with landscape gardeners working on a grand scale, particularly for the approach to a country house. In 'The Gardener's Prayer' Sir George Douglas wrote:

On whirling winglets for a while up-borne,
Your travelling lime-tree-seed
Parent of groves whose fronts shall greet the morn
Light on the verdant mead!

A splendid double avenue can be seen at Clumber Park in Nottinghamshire. The protection the lime afforded is referred to by William Shakespeare in *The Tempest* although he uses the old name, *line:*

All prisoners, sir,
In the Line grove, which weather-fends your cell

According to a statute of Edward I trees were required to be planted in churchyards to 'defend the church from high winds'. The clergy were allowed to cut them down in order to repair the chancel, when necessary. The lime and the elm were often preferred to the slow-growing yew. From the inner bark, according to Philemon Holland's *Pliny's Natural History* 'there bee thin pellicles or skins lying in many folds together, whereof are made bands and cords called Bazen ropes'. The inner bark, known as bast, was used by gardeners for tying up plants and by furniture dealers for packing goods; lime subsequently acquired the name baste-tree.

In folk lore lime is a symbol of wedded love, an attribute it may have acquired through the legend of a humble shepherd, Philemon, and his wife Baucis, who lived in a Phrygian village. They shared their meagre food with the gods Hermes and Zeus when, disguised as humans, they were unable to find shelter for the night. As a reward for their kindness Zeus granted their wish that in due course, they would die together. Philemon became an oak, a symbol of hospitality, and Baucis a lime, the emblem of conjugal affection. In due course the topmost branches of each tree became entwined. Jonathan Swift commemorated this story thus:

Kindly did the gods invite
To his poor hut to pass the night;
And then the hospitable sire
Bid Goody Baucis mend the fire.

In plant lore lime is the birthday flower for 7 February and symbolizes fidelity, gentleness, hospitality, modesty, pliancy and sweetness. Because it separates into several stems at the ground it is symbolic of a capacity for several simultaneous lines of thought. Sitting under the tree was thought to be beneficial. It may have inspired the poet Samuel Coleridge, who, unable to join his visitors, having met with an accident before their arrival (June 1797), composed 'This Lime-Tree Bower My Prison' as he sat beneath the tree awaiting their return from a walk.

This little lime-tree bower, have I not marked
Much that has soothed me. Pale beneath the blaze
Hung the transparent foliage; and I watched
Some broad and sunny leaf, and loved to see
The shadow of the leaf and stem above
Dappling its sunshine!

Nevertheless the more superstitious folk believed the lime to be a life index tree for the family who owned it. A fallen branch foretold a death in that family.

In Roman antiquity garlands were tied with a bark of the lime and worn at feasts to prevent intoxication and in Greek mythology the dryades or wood nymphs were wedded to the lime tree. The trembling of the leaves in the wind displaying much of their under surface, was regarded in country lore as a sign of rain. However, the explanation may be in the fact that the damp air softens the leaf stalk.

The new soft green leaves of the lime, which should be picked whilst the shell-pink scale leaves still cling to the opened leaf buds, were used to make an unusual sandwich filling with a sprinkling of lemon juice or a layer of cream cheese. The blossom gathered in July and lightly dried was said to produce a fragrant and refreshing tea which also reputedly induced sweat in fevers. The flowers were used in a cure for epilepsy. Herbalists steeped the bark of the tree in water until a thick mucilaginous substance formed, which was applied to burns and scalds. The leaves, boiled in water, provided a lotion to treat ulcers, sores, wrinkles, freckles and other skin complaints.

MEDLAR

And as I stood and cast aside mine eye,
I was 'ware of the fairest medlar tree
That ever yet in all my life I see,
As full of blossomes as it might be.
Therein a goldfinch leaping prettily
From bough to bough, and, as him list, he eat
Here and there, of buds and flowers sweet.
'The Flower and The Leaf' ANON (Fifteenth century)

MEDLAR (*Mespilus germanica*). The generic name is from the Greek *mesos*, meaning half, and *pilos*, meaning ball, in reference to the shape of the fruit, which is not unlike a giant pinkish-brown rosehip with a deep hollow at one end surrounded by long withered sepals. A single white flower appears at the end of each short leafy twig in early summer. Medlar is a native of south-east Europe and south-west Asia but it has been so long established in England that it is now completely naturalized.

This low-growing picturesque tree (which is excellent for shade), with its contorted trunk, is more often grown nowadays as an unusual ornamental addition to the lawn of a flower garden. In earlier times, when it was prized as a more desirable fruit it was a great favourite and included with quince, walnut and mulberry in the corners of herb gardens and orchards. However, it no longer enjoys such popularity. Wild specimens of medlar can still be found in south-east England.

In the warmer regions of the Mediterranean the fruit can be eaten from the tree but in our climate they are only edible when 'bletted' – that is, when they have become over-ripe to the point that the flesh softens, but before the outer skin shows sign of decay. If the fruit is left on the tree an early frost will start the process.

> *...that true child of Fall, whose morbid fruit*
> *Ripens, with walnuts, only in November,*
> *The Medlar lying brown across the thatch;*
> *Rough elbows of rough branches, russet fruit*
> *So blet it's worth no more than sleepy pear,*
> *But in its motley pink and yellow leaf*
> *A harlequin that some may overlook*

wrote Vita Sackville-West in 'The Garden'. The fruit can be picked in early autumn and laid out under cover for two or three weeks to soften. An alternative method, according to *Child's Guide* (1850) advised that 'they are kept in moist bran for a fortnight before being rotten enough to eat'. Medlar taste rather like baked apple and can be cooked in a similar way in a shallow dish with cloves and butter, and eaten directly out of their skin with a spoon. Some enthusiasts eat them as a dessert by separating the squashy centre from the outer skin and mixing it with cream and sugar. They were also used in jellies and for preserves and fillings for pies. The need to allow the fruit to 'blet' was familiar to the audiences of Shakespeare, who, when he described the fruit as only fit to be eaten when rotten was using the common language of the day. In *Measure for Measure* he writes

> *They would have married me to the rotten Medlar*

and in *As You Like It* Rosalind tells the clown Touchstone:

> *I'll graff it with you, and then I shall graff it with a Medlar;*
> *then it will be the earliest fruit in the country, for you'll be*
> *rotten ere you behalf ripe, and that's the right virtue of the*
> *Medlar.*

The tree is also mentioned in *Romeo and Juliet*:

> *Now will he sit under a Medlar tree,*
> *And wish his mistress were that kind of fruit*
> *As maids call Medlars when they laugh alone*

Herbalists attributed various medicinal virtues to the medlar fruit, particularly as an aid to improving the memory. The Elizabethan herbalist Culpepper advised 'the fruit is Saturn's, and there is no better medicine to strengthen the retentive faculty'. The fruit was recommended to be eaten during pregnancy 'to stay the longings after unusual meats, and prevent miscarriage'. A plaster made of the dried fruit and applied to the back was helpful too. A decoction of the fruit was used as a gargle to treat painful swellings or blood in the mouth and throat. A poultice or plaster consisting of dried medlars mixed with the juice of red roses, a few cloves, nutmeg and a little red coral was applied to the stomach to cure the pain caused by eating meat. The leaves, dried and powdered, were sprinkled on wounds to staunch the flow of blood and heal the injury. Medlar stones powdered and drunk in wine in which parsley roots had been infused were recommended for expelling kidney stones.

MULBERRY

The Mulberry tree was hung with blooming wreaths;
The Mulberry tree stood centre of the dance;
The Mulberry tree was hymn'd with dulcet strains;
And from his touchwood trunk the Mulberry tree
Supplied such relics as devotion holds
Still scared, and preserves with pious care.
'The Task' WILLIAM COWPER

MULBERRY (*Morus nigra*). The generic name is Latin for the tree, although older writers claim that it is a Greek word for fool; *nigra* simply means black. However, there is a white variety which is distinguished by its shiny leaf and white or pinkish fruit. The black mulberry was introduced to Europe by the Romans who ate mulberries at their feasts. Pliny wrote of its use in medicine adding, 'Of all the cultivated trees, the Mulberry is the last that buds, which it never does until cold weather is past, and it is therefore called the wisest of trees. But when it begins to put forth buds, it dispatches the business in one night, and that with so much force, that their breaking forth may be evidently heard.' The fruit, which has a bitter taste, does not seem to have been cultivated in England before 1550. Nevertheless in Anglo-Saxon times, morat, a compound of honey flavoured with mulberries, was said to be a favourite drink. Sir Walter Scott mentions it in *Ivanhoe* although other sources suggest there could have been some confusion with blackberries. Edmund Spenser also wrote of the fruit in 'Elegy':

With love juice stained the Mulberie
The fruit that dewes the poet's braine.

Henry Lyte, author of *A Nievve Herbal* (1619) wrote: 'It is called in the fayning of the Poetes the wisest of all other trees, for this tree only among all others bringeth forth his leaves after the cold frostes be past.' John Gerard described the tree as 'high and full of boughes' and added that it grew in his London garden. He advised 'that the barke of the root is bitter, hot and drie … it purgeth the belly, and driveth forth worms.' According to Cunningham's *Handbook of London*, Mulberry Garden, mentioned by old dramatists, 'occupied the site of the present Buckingham Palace and Gardens, and derived its name from a garden of Mulberry trees planted by King James I in 1609' The king encouraged the planting of quantities of black mulberry in error. He hoped to feed silkworms with the mulberry in an effort to establish a silk industry in England. Unfortunately the worms prefer the white mulberry (*morus alba*), a native of China which does not grow well in England. Nevertheless the mulberry was a much prized ornament in established gardens and 'on the lawn is a patent of nobility to any garden; and is most easy of cultivation' – according to Rev Henry Ellacombe. Ellacombe also wrote of the ease of propagation, telling of a Mr Payne Knight cutting large branches from a mulberry tree to make standards for his clothes lines. Each took root and became a flourishing tree. Proof of Shakespeare's familiarity with the tree can be found in the so called Shakespeare Mulberry that grew in his garden at New Place, Stratford-on-Avon. According to Edmund Malone (1741–1812), the Irish editor of Shakespeare, who published an eleven-volume edition of the great dramatist in 1890, 'That Shakespeare planted this tree is as well authenticated as anything of that nature can be … and till this was planted there was no Mulberry tree in the neighbourhood. The tree was celebrated in many a poem, one especially by Dibdin, but in about 1752, the then new owner of New Place, the Rev Gastrell,

bought and pulled down the house, and wishing, as it should seem, to be 'damned to everlasting fame', he cut down Shakespeare's celebrated Mulberry tree, to save himself the trouble of showing it to those 'whose admiration of our great poet led them to visit the poetick ground on which it stood.' The pieces of wood were either made into snuff boxes, some inscribed with the punning motto 'Memento Mori', or other keepsakes. As with all fruit wood, mulberry is hard and difficult to carve. According to wood carver Trevor Ellis, who recently restored much of Grinling Gibbons' exquisite work at Hampton Court, the wood is the colour of English mustard in the early stages but within six months changes to horse chestnut. It is now quite rare and only available in small pieces.

William Shakespeare's plays contain several references to the fruit; for example in *Coriolanus*:

> *Thy stout heart*
> *Now humble as the ripest Mulberry*
> *That will not bear handling.*

And another in *A Midsummer Night's Dream*:

> *Feed him with Apricocks and Dewberries,*
> *With purple Grapes, green Figs, and Mulberries.*
> *And Thisbe tarrying in Mulberry shade.*

This is a reference to the classical legend of Pyramus and Thisbe. The fruit of all mulberry trees was originally white, but was darkened by the blood of Thisbe and Pyramus whose deaths arose out of a tragic misunderstanding. Thisbe had arranged to meet her love Pyramus, near a white mulberry tree. Arriving early she was startled by a lion and fled dropping her veil, which the animal smeared with blood as it wandered along. On finding the veil Pyramus thought Thisbe was dead and so killed himself. When Thisbe returned and discovered his body she stabbed herself in her grief. The blood of the lovers was said to have changed the colour of the berries. In 1769, when the famous actor and dramatist David Garrick received the Freedom of Stratford-upon-Avon, the key was in a carved box said to be made from the original mulberry tree. A cup was also made, which Garrick held while he sang one of his own compositions, on the occasion of Shakespeare's Jubilee :

All shall kneel to the Mulberry tree;
Bend to the blest Mulberry;
Matchless was he who planted thee;
And thou like him immortal shall be.

In plant lore a mulberry tree is the birthday emblem for 19 June and symbolizes kindliness offset by sharpness or wisdom. Black mulberry is the birthday flower for 20 June and in the language of the flowers means 'I shall not survive you'. According to Culpepper Mercury rules the tree. He commented that 'it is so well known where it groweth, that it needeth no description.' He recommended the leaves for treating haemorrhoids, bleeding from the mouth and also nose wounds. Soaked in vinegar the leaves were applied to burns. A decoction of the leaves and bark was used as a mouthwash and for toothache and the juice from the berries was said to cure inflammations or sores in the mouth or throat, and 'palate when it is fallen down'.

John Parkinson (1567–1650), apothecary and author of *Paradisus Terrestris*, was none too complimentary on the subject of mulberries: 'they stain the fingers and lips that eat them, and do quickly putrefie in the stomach, if they be taken before meat.' Nevertheless, more recently the fruit was used to flavour or colour syrups.

'Here we go round the mulberry bush' is an old game in which children join hands and dance around in a circle, singing. It is said to have originated from prisoners' daily exercise around a mulberry tree in their prison yard.

OAK

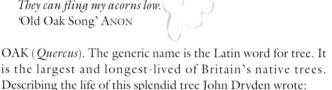

My growth is slow
Up and below.
My roots hold fast,
I shall last,
I shall last
As long as the wild winds know
They can fling my acorns low.
'Old Oak Song' ANON

OAK (*Quercus*). The generic name is the Latin word for tree. It is the largest and longest-lived of Britain's native trees. Describing the life of this splendid tree John Dryden wrote:

The monarch oak, the patriarch of the trees,
Shoots rising up, and spreads by slow degree;
Three centuries he grows, and three he stays
Supreme in state, and in three more decays.

Evidence of the great oak plantations of the past can still be seen today in the New Forest and the Forest of Dean, although there are many individual trees and forests representing daring deeds and legends throughout the country – for example, Robin Hood and his association with Sherwood Forest. Oaks, in the past, were often used to mark the boundaries of English parishes and it was customary for the local dignitaries and villagers to walk these boundaries once a year reciting passages from the gospel. Robert Herrick appeared to have had strong feelings about this custom:

Dearest, bury me
Under the holy oak, or gospel tree
Where though thou see'st not thou may'st think upon
Me, when thou goest Procession.

The unfurling of the leaves in the spring indicated its use as a weather oracle (see Ash), and an abundance of acorns suggested a long harsh winter. For centuries the hard, durable timber of the oak has been used in ship building. Barry Cornwall wrote:

Thou O Oak! the strong ship-builder,
For thy country's good
Givest up thy noble life,
Like a patriot in the strife.

'Hearts of oak are our ships, hearts of oak are our men!' are familiar lines from an old patriotic song. The wood has always been used for making furniture, often embellished with ornate carvings, particularly in churches. An old rhyme suggests that the fallen leaves were used in an old New Year's Eve custom:

From the wood some oak leaves bring
That were green in early spring;
Scatter them about the bier
Of the now departing year.

In plant lore the oak is a symbol of courage, independence, faith, longevity, fire, royalty, stability, honour and reward. It is the birthday emblem for 24 January and signifies bravery, flames, humanity and welcome. The tree was sacred to the sky and thunder gods, particularly Jupiter, the supreme deity of Roman mythology, and for this reason it was known as Jove's tree. As it was his tree it was believed that it could not be struck by lightning in a storm:

Strike Elm, strike Rowan
Not the Oak.

The Greeks dedicated the tree to Zeus – his oracle was located in a grove of oaks. Our ancestors worshipped the oak in the belief that it was the first tree created, and one of the oldest means of divination was to interpret the voice of the supreme deity through the rustling of its branches. The Druids, priests of the ancient Britons, venerated the oak, wearing leaves round their brows as they worshipped under the trees, keeping a fire burning of oak timber, in honour of their god; once a year the followers lit their fires from its sacred flame. Before searching for mistletoe, which they also venerated, a sacrifice was made of white bull killed with a golden sickle:

The fearless British priests, under the aged oak,
Taking a milk-white bull, unstained with the yoke,
And with an axe of gold, from that Jove-sacred tree
The Mistletoe cut down.

The mistletoe was later distributed among the worshippers, to be suspended in their homes to ward off evil spirits. They believed that the berries were the fertilizing dew of the supreme deity. In earlier times the felling of an oak tree caused a death – such legends and associations lingered on through the years. The oak is a symbol of England and formed the badge of the Stuarts. Formerly a sprig of oak leaves and oak apples were worn in button holes and caps on the 29 May to commemorate the birthday of Charles II who hid in an oak at Boscobel, after the Battle of Worcester (3 September 1651). An Act of Parliament in 1664 ordered the day to be observed as one of thanksgiving. A childhood rhyme still chanted in fairly recent times by schoolchildren, recalls the custom – those not wearing the emblem paid a forfeit.

> *Royal Oak Day*
> *The 29th of May*
> *If you don't give us a holiday*
> *We will run away*

Herbalists found the oak quite useful. The water found in the hollow places of old oaks was recommended as effective against 'foul spread scabs' while the bark, leaves and powdered acorn cups were said by Culpepper 'to bind and dry very much'. The inner bark of the tree and the thin skin covering the acorn was advised for those spitting blood while the bark and powdered acorn, made into milk, was said to be an antidote to poisonous herbs and medicine. The acorn powdered and taken in wine was an effective diuretic and the distilled water of the oak bud, before it has broken into leaf was used 'inwardly and outwardly to assuage inflammations, and stop all manner of fluxes'. Acorns have been ground up in the past in times of great need as a substitute for flour, but records show they were more usually used to feed pigs. Although medieval porkers probably ate mainly earth and pignuts, advice concerning acorns was to hand:

> *Though good store of acorns the porkling do fat*
> *Not taken in season may perish of that,*
> *If pig do start rattling and choking in throat*
> *Thou loosest thy porkling – a pig to a groat!*

OLIVE

And still the olive spreads its foliage round
Morea's fallen sanctuaries and towers,
Once its green boughs Minerva's votaries crown'd
Deem'd a meet offering for celestial powers.
'Modern Greece' FELICIA HEMANS

OLIVE (*Olea europaea*). The olive is an evergreen tree which can attain a height of forty feet. Although they grow well in sub-tropical areas, in England they do need a long hot summer for the fruits to ripen fully. The fruit can be gathered green or when they are fully ripe and have turned black. Nevertheless they do need suitable growing conditions to attain a great age. Uncertainty surrounds the introduction of the olive tree to England, but in a translation from the Anglo-Saxon *Leech Book* of the tenth century there is a prescription: 'Pound lovage and elder rind and oleaster, that is wild olive, mix them with some clear ale and give to drink.' So there is a strong probability that the tree was introduced by the Romans.

John Parkinson knew it as an English tree, writing in his *Herball* (1640): 'It flowereth in the beginning of summer in the warmer countries, but very late with us; the fruite ripeneth in autumne in Spain,&c., but seldome with us.' Miller, author of *Account of Gardens Round London* (1691), writes that the earliest date that he could discover was 1648, at which time it was grown in the Oxford Botanic Garden. In earlier times one can safely conclude that although the association of the olive branch with Noah and the Flood was known to many, very few people in Britain had actually seen the tree. The writer and painter John Ruskin described it perfectly: 'the Olive is one of the most characteristic and beautiful features of all southern scenery ... What the Elm and the Oak are to England, the

Olive is to Italy ... It had been well for painters to have felt and seen the Olive tree, to have loved it for Christ's sake ... to have loved it even to the hoary dimness of its delicate foliage, subdued and faint of hue ...to have traced line by line the gnarled writhings of its intricate branches and the pointed fretwork of its light and narrow leaves ... and the rosy white stars of its spring blossoming, and the heads of sable fruit scattered by autumn along its topmost bough. Although it is greatly admired abroad it is not often grown in England even as an ornamental tree.'

In plant lore olive is the birthday flower for 8 March and is symbolic of faith, fecundity, good tidings, hope, long life, liberty, mercy, mirth, peace, perception of divine love, preservation, prosperity, reconciliation, security, supplication, victory and wisdom. In Christianity it is sacred to the saints Bernard of Tolomei and Pantaleon and also St Agnes who is usually represented as holding in her hand a palm branch, while at her feet or in her arms is a lamb (*agnus*). She is sometimes crowned with olives and holding an olive branch as well as the palm. In the Bible a garland of olives was given to Judith when she restored peace to the Israelites after the death of Holofernes. 'And they put a garland of olive upon her, and she went before all the people in the dance, leading all the women; and all the men of Israel followed in their armour, with garlands, and songs in their mouths.'

Olive land was one of the names of Egypt, and Horus, the supreme god to the early immigrants to that country, was called child of the olive tree. Olive has always been a symbol of peace among the Jews, Greeks and Romans. In the Bible there is a reference to an olive wreath set on the head of an ox that went before the bearers of first fruits to Jerusalem to be offered as a sacrifice of peace. The Mount of Olives is nearby. At New Year the Greeks took a branch of the olive tree to their neighbours as a token of goodwill; even ambassadors bore them in their hand as an expression of peaceful intentions. (In the historic gardens of Greece the olive is pre-eminent.) Shakespeare makes at least eight references to either a branch or crown of olives in his plays and in most instances refers to the symbolic meaning. In *Anthony and Cleopatra* Caesar says:

> *Prove this prosperous day, the thrice-mocked world*
> *Shall bear the olive freely.*

In *Timon of Athens*, he suggests a sword wreathed with olive can do no harm:

> *Bring me into your city, And I will use the olive with my sword*

An olive grove is suggested in *As You Like It*:

> *Where, in the purlieus of this forest stands*
> *A sheepcote fenced about with Olive trees?*

In Roman mythology olive is sacred to the god Jupiter and the goddess Minerva, who in Greek mythology equates with Athena. According to legend she struck the ground and an olive tree sprang up. Edmund Spenser paid homage to this story when he wrote:

With her weapon dread
She smote upon the ground, the which straight forth did yield
A fruitful olive tree with berries spread

The olive was judged to be a greater gift to mankind than Poseidon's gift of a horse, and the city of Athens was named after her. At public games the conquerors and heroes were crowned with wreaths of leaves. At the Olympic Games the garlands were made of wild olive. An olive branch was also the highest award to a citizen.

The beautifully grained wood not only takes a fine polish but is faintly fragrant and was used for small cabinet work and in earlier times carved into statues of gods. Planted in groves – a breathtaking prospect – the olive tree bears fruit in its second year 'and repays cultivation in its sixth', continuing as a source of wealth even when old and hollow. The ripe fruits, which are delicious, are pressed to extract the oil although the method varies in different countries. Virgin oil, which has a greenish tint, is of very good quality, is excellent for cooking and as the basis for salad dressings and is a valuable asset to a healthy diet. It was formerly used as a laxative, to relieve the effects of burns and stings and was considered invaluable as a lubricant in skin and muscular complaints, chest and abdominal chills, scarlet fever, typhoid, plague and dropsy.

ORANGE

Where the orange blossom blow,
Where the blooms are white as snow,
There is one sweet song for me;
It is borne across the lea,
Some fruit for him that dressed me.
Bathed in a wreath of light:
Where orange blooms are bright.
'Orange Blossom' ELLA MARY GORDON

ORANGE (*Citrus sinensis*) is a sweet variety. Oranges grow well in warm, virtually frost-free areas, such as the Mediterranean countries, as Leigh Hunt (1784–1859) recalls in 'An Italian Garden':

With orange, whose warm leaves so finely suit,
And look as if they shade a golden fruit

They often produce two crops a year and may bear flowers at the same time as an earlier orange crop is maturing. In England, they require considerably more attention. The seed may be grown under cover in a bed of nutrient rich compost, or in a container, but will not necessarily bear fruit. The handsome evergreen foliage, sweetly scented delicate white flowers and the fruit were described by Alfred, Lord Tennyson as:

A fruit of pure Hesperian gold
That smelled ambrosially.

Orange trees were greatly admired in earlier times. In Miller's *Account of Gardens Round London* in 1691, they were described as if always under glass, although an account is given 'of the first trees at Beddington, that were planted in the open ground, under a movable covert during the winter months;

that they always bore fruit in great plenty and perfection; that they grew on the south side of a wall, not nailed against it, but at full liberty to spread. They were killed entirely by the great frost in 1739–40.' In 1554 John Evelyn described them as having been 'planted in the naked earth one hundred years since'. The poet Andrew Marvell wrote of their beauty in 'Bermudas':

The Orange bright,
Like golden lamps in a green night.

In Christian art the orange is an attribute of the Virgin Mary and in plant lore, a celestial fruit symbolic of feminine principle, generosity, infinity and perfection. An orange tree symbolizes southern countries. Orange blossom is the birthday flower for 26 January and signifies chastity, eternal love and fertility. In the language of the flowers it means 'You are pure and worthy.' It is a nuptial flower that must be discarded before it withers or it will bring barrenness.

Youths and enamoured maidens vie to wear
This flower, their bosoms grace, or curled amid their hair

wrote Catullus (c.87–54 BC). Tennyson alludes to the delightful custom, introduced from France in about 1820, of a bride carrying orange blossom as her wedding bouquet:

Like a bride of old
In triumph led
With music and sweet showers
Of festal flowers
Unto the dwelling she must away.

In mythology the orange is associated with Zeus and Hera (king and queen of the sky) and alleged to be the golden apples presented by Gaea (earth) as a wedding gift. These apples could only be grown in the gardens of the Hesperides where they were protected by three nymphs and Ladon, a very dangerous non-sleeping dragon. It was the eleventh labour of Hercules to obtain some of these golden apples. He succeeded but as they could not be preserved elsewhere they were carried back by Minerva. The orange is said to indicate hope of fruitfulness, as few trees are more prolific, while the white blossoms are symbolic of innocence. The phrase 'go gathering orange blossom' suggests looking for a wife. Shakespeare refers several times to the colour of the orange and in *Much Ado About Nothing* to the disposition of the fruit:

The count is neither sad nor sick, nor merry nor well; but civil count, civil as an Orange, and something of that jealous complexion.

Commercially, the orange was imported on a grand scale, mainly as a dessert fruit or for marmalade, although John Parkinson, while making no mention of the fruit being eaten raw said 'they are used as a sauce for many sorts of meats, in respect of the sweet sourness giving a relish and delight whereinsoever they are used'. He also recommended that when the seeds have grown a finger length in height they give 'a fine and aromatick or spicy taste, very acceptable among Sallats.' Amongst her numerous recipes for oranges, which range through fritters, puddings and preserves, Mrs Beeton recommended orange wine through a simple and easy method of making a 'very superior' nine gallons, consisting of ninety Seville oranges, 32 lbs of lump sugar and water, for the equivalent, at that time of ten pence. A popular nightcap, known as a bishop, consisted of half a pint of water with small quantities of cinnamon, cloves, mace, allspice and a race of ginger root boiled until reduced by half. A bottle of port wine was heated and the spicy liquid added to a roasted orange pricked with cloves. A few sugar lumps, rind of lemon and grated nutmeg completed the recipe for this mulled wine which was served hot. As Jonathan Swift remarked:

> *Fine orange well roasted, with wine in a cup,*
> *They'll make a sweet bishop when gentlefolks sup.*

Pomanders, consisting of an orange pierced with cloves, dried, and tied with ribbons, sometimes enclosed in a hinged, decorative silver ball, were carried by our ancestors to divert sensitive noses from the unpleasant odours emanating from the unhygienic conditions of the day. In more recent times the fruit was an important 'surprise' gift amongst the contents of a Christmas stocking. Childhood days link the fruit with the lemon in the delightful rhyme game 'Oranges and Lemons':

> *Oranges and lemons, say the bells of St Clement's,*
> *You owe me five farthings, say the bells of St Martin's.*
> *When will you pay me, say the bells of Old Bailey.*
> *When I grow rich, say the bells of Shoreditch.*
> *Here comes the candle to light you to bed,*
> *And here comes a chopper to chop off your head.*
> *Chop! Chop! the last man's head!*

PEACH

Graceful and young, the peach tree stands;
How rich its flowers, all gleaming bright
This bride to her new home repairs;
Chamber and house she'll order right.
Chinese poem translated by Dr Legge

PEACH (*Prunus persica*). The generic name is also Latin for cherry and plum; *persica* means Persian. Peach has been culti-vated for centuries in most parts of Asia and as its name sug-gests was introduced to Europe from Persia (Iran). According to Mrs Grieve's *Modern Herbal* uncertainty surrounds its intro-duction to Greece but it is suggested that the Romans brought it direct from Persia during the reign of Emperor Claudius I (10BC–54AD). When it was first introduced it was known as *Malus persica* or Persian apple. The expedition of Alexander had made it known to Theophrastus, who in 392 BC, spoke of it as the Persian fruit. As we know it, the peach has never been found in a wild state and some authorities believed it to be of Chinese origin, as it is mentioned in the books of Confucius, and the antiquity and knowledge of the fruit is represented in sculpture and on porcelain. Some naturalists, including Charles Darwin, thought it was a modification of the almond and it was classed with that fruit as a distinct genus. The fruit, known as a drupe, has a similar structure to that of the plum and the apri-cot. The name peach occurs in Archbishop Aelfric's *Vocabulary* in the tenth century as 'Persicarius, Pereseoctreow' and it is claimed that John de Garlande grew it in the thirteenth centu-ry. What is certain is that it has been cultivated in England since the early part of the sixteenth century. John Gerard refers to several varieties growing in his garden including a 'double-flowered peach' which was also grown by John Parkinson, author of *Paradisus Terrestris* (1629) – the title being a pun on his own name, Park-in-sun (which was the first illustrated book devoted primarily to ornamental plants. In his book, *Emblems*, Henry Peacham (1576–1642) describes the rich variety of fruit to be seen in an English garden:

> *The Persian peach and fruitful quince,*
> *And there the forward almond grieve,*
> *With cherries knowne no long time since,*
> *The winder warden, orchards pride,*
> *The philbert that loves the wall,*
> *And red apple, so envied*
> *Of school boys passing by the pole.*

Vita Sackville-West, mindful of 'the hated wasp' viewed the peach by moonlight in 'Summer in The Garden':

> *… I sought*
> *The rosy rondure of the moonlight peach*
> *So stilly heavy on her slender twig,*
> *Too often out of reach.*

Peach is generally cultivated either under cover where it is best fan-trained or grown against a sunny sheltered wall – both require pruning in early spring and summer. It can, however, be grown as an ornamental tree to be appreciated simply for the beauty of its spring blossom. The fruit is harvested when fully ripe; a good indication of this is to rest the fruit in the palm of the hand and apply gentle pressure with one's thumb on the part of the peach near the stalk. In warmer climates orchards consisting of thousands of trees are a wonderful sight to behold. The American author of children's verse, Eugene Field, wrote of the fruit:

> *A little peach in an orchard grew*
> *A little peach of emerald hue;*
> *Warmed by the sun and wet by the dew,*
> *It grew.*

Peach was considered to be a great delicacy in Shakespeare's

time but he only refers to it by the colour of the blossom: 'To take note how many pairs of silk stockings thou hast, viz, these, and those that were thy Peach-coloured ones!' in *Henry IV, Part II* and in *Measure for Measure* '… for some four suits of Peach-coloured satin, which now peaches him a beggar'. The poet Andrew Marvell, in 'Garden Thoughts', described how:

> *The nectarines and curious peach*
> *Into my hands themselves do reach.*

In plant lore peach blossom, which is assigned to the planet Venus, is the birthday flower for 25 April and symbolizes a bride and the season of spring. In the language of the flowers it signifies 'I am your captive.' The leaves, bark, flowers and kernels all contributed towards a valuable medicine chest. Early herbalists applied fresh leaves as a poultice which was applied externally to the body to expel worms and an infusion of the leaves was taken for the same purpose. Culpepper advised that the powdered leaves 'strewed on fresh bleeding wounds stayeth their bleeding and closeth them.' A syrup and an infusion of peach flowers was recommended by Gerard as a mild purgative and for jaundice – particularly for children and the infirm. A cure for baldness, which has occupied great minds for centuries, was said to be found in an application of peach kernel boiled in vinegar. The kernels mixed with honey were recommended as a tonic. Peach flowers steeped overnight in wine produced a pleasant laxative and a tincture of the flowers was said to allay the pain of colic. One was advised to collect peach leaves for drying in June and July.

PEAR

PEAR (*Pyrus communis*). The generic name is Latin for pear.
The common or wild pear was probably first introduced to
Britain by the Romans, followed by other varieties from
Europe where it had been established for centuries. The origin
of the tree is western Asia. The truly wild pear is most likely an
escapee from the orchards of earlier times. Pear was one of the
six most common trees mentioned in Anglo-Saxon charters as
boundary features. In spring the pear tree, whether it is
upright, displaying its pyramidal shape or espaliered on a stone
wall, is a magnificent sight draped in its snow-white blossom –
a beautiful ornament in any garden or orchard. It was the har-
vesting of the fruit which concerned Thomas Tusser
(1520–80), the English writer on agriculture and author of *A
Hundreth Goode Pointes of Husbandrie* who advised:

Fruit gathered too timely will taste of the wood,
will shrink and be bitter; and seldom prove good:
so fruit that is shaken, and beat off a tree,
with bruising in falling, soon faulty will be.

The popularity of the pear was quite evident by the Tudor period. John Gerard, the Elizabethan herbalist and gardener, noted
that there were so many different kinds of the fruit that 'the
stocke or kindred of Pears are not to be numbered; every coun-

try hath his peculiar fruit, so that to describe them apart were to send an owle to Athens, or to number those things that are without number'.

In *All's Well That Ends Well* Shakespeare is particularly disparaging about foreign varieties:

> *Your virginity, your old virginity, is like one of our*
> *French withered Pears, it looks ill, it eats drily; marry,*
> *'tis a withered Pear; it was formerly better; marry, yet*
> *'tis a withered Pear.*

He does however, mention two pears by name: Poperin and Warden: 'O, Romeo … thou a Poperin Pear', and in *A Winter's Tale*: 'I must have Saffron to colour the Warden pies'(cochineal and red wine replaced saffron). The Warden Pear originates from the horticultural skills of the twelfth century Cistercian Monks of Warden Abbey in Bedfordshire. Other sources suggest the name is derived from Old French, *wardant* or keeping. The pears were a traditional local delicacy, sold on the Feast of St Simon and St Jude (28 October) accompanied by the cry:

> *Who knows what I have got?*
> *In a pot hot?*
> *Baked wardens … all are hot*
> *Who knows what I have got?*

John Parkinson, the apothecary to James I, whose *Theatrum Botanicum* was once the most comprehensive English book on medicinal plants, observed 'The Warden or Lukewards Pear are two sorts, both white and red, both great and small.' The latter name seems perhaps to suggest that St Luke's Day (18 October) was the day to pick the fruit. Parkinson also mentions the Poperin: 'The summer Popperin and the winter Popperin, both of them very good, firm, dry Pears, somewhat spotted and brownish on the outside.' Sources suggest it was probably a Flemish pear introduced by the antiquary Leland who was made Rector of Popering by Henry VIII:

> *His name was Sir Thomas*
> *Alone he was in fer contre,*
> *In Flaundres, all beyonde the se,*
> *At Popering in the place.*

From the Choke-pear, which has a rough astringent taste, came the custom of referring to anything that stopped speech, such as an unanswerable argument or a biting remark, as a choke-pear. In *Clarissa* Samuel Richardson wrote 'Pardon me for going so low as to talk of giving choke-pears' and 'He gave him a choake-peare to stoppe his breath' is found in *Euphues* by John Lyly (c.1554–1606). Dr Prior, author of *Popular Names of British Plants* thought it could be an allusion to the death of Emperor Claudius' son, Druscus, who choked on a pear. The Catherine pear was also popular and was probably named after St Catherine, the martyr, whose feast day falls on 25 November. The poet John Suckling (1609–42) compares a bride's cheeks to the colour of the fruit in his 'Ballad upon Weddings':

> *For streaks of red were mingled there*
> *Such as are on a Catherine pear (the side that's next the sun).*

He continued on an amusing note:

> *Her lips were red, and one was thin*
> *Compared to that was next her chin (Some bee had stung it*
> *newly).*

Tradition has it that King John was poisoned by an unknown ingredient (possibly fungi), which was added to a dish of pears

given to him by the monks of Swinstead Abbey. According to *A Suffolk Calendar* the first appearance of the fruit indicated the quality of the crop:

If St Margaret [20 July] *brings the first pear*
Pears will abound for the rest of the year.

However, there were those who believed in the old saying:

A pear year,
A dear year.

In folk lore a pear tree symbolizes comfort and in many parts of the world is held sacred because of its pyramidal form. The pear represents the human heart. In Christianity it typifies Christ's love for mankind. Pear blossom is the birthday flower for 17 August and symbolizes affection. In the language of the flowers it means 'not altogether lovely'. Culpepper advised his readers that 'the tree belongs to Venus. For their physical use they are best discerned by their taste. All the sweet and luscious sorts … help to move the belly downwards, more or less. Those that are hard and sour, bind the belly as much and the leaves do also.' He also stated that 'the harsher sorts' were more beneficial in healing wounds and cooling the blood. Pear boiled with honey was advised for the 'oppressed stomach'.Cooked with mushrooms, pear is believed to act as an antidote if a poisonous mushroom is accidentally included in the dish.

A well sunk close to a wild pear tree was said to produce water that would cure gout. Pear orchards still produce the refreshing beverage, perry, introduced by the Normans and similar in taste to cider. The wood is hard and easily stained and polished, consequently it is used for musical instruments, veneers and carvings.

SCOTS PINE

This is the forest primeval.
The murmuring pines and hemlock,
Bearded with moss, and with garments green,
Indistinct in the twilight,
Stand like Druids of old, with voices sad and prophetic.
'The Wail of the Forest' H.W. LONGFELLOW

SCOTS PINE (*Pinus sylvestris*). The generic name is the Latin word for pine. In the early vocabularies it is called *pintreow* and the cones, *pin-nuttes*. They were also known as pine-apples. The name was transferred to the West Indian fruit from its similarity to a fir-cone, although it was still in use in medieval times. The Scots pine, commonly but incorrectly known as Scotch fir, is a typical pine tree of Northern Europe with its straight, unbranched, cylindrical trunk. The Scots pine was the only large conifer able to re-emerge from the ravages of the Ice Age in northern Britain. Today the forests still retain a gracious but unfortunately limited presence due to earlier exploitation of the

Scottish Highlands. The rivers and lochs provided a natural highway for the supply of pine for planks and ship masts in the dockyards. Alfred, Lord Tennyson wrote:

They came, they cut away my tallest Pines
My dark tall Pines, that plumed the craggy ledge.
High o'er the blue gorge, and all between
The snowy peak and snow white cataract
Fostered the callow eaglet

The Scots pine does grow elsewhere although it is only in the Highlands that it can be regarded as wild and indigenous, as the red squirrel knows to its cost; efforts are being made to redress this imbalance. As to be expected, pine is the emblem of many Scottish clans and Sir Walter Scott (1771–1832) refers to one in particular in 'The Boat Song of the McGregors':

Hail to the chief who in triumph advances,
Honour'd and bless'd be the evergreen pine!
Long may the tree in his banner that glances
Flourish the shelter and grace of our line!

In plant lore pine is the birthday flower for 21 March and symbolizes boldness, endurance, fidelity, immortality and health.

The vitality of the tree is believed to have the power to strengthen the soul of the deceased and to preserve the body from corruption. Twin pines signify fidelity and passionate love. The pine cone is sacred to love goddesses and symbolizes abundance, fecundity, fire, good luck, life, phallic principle and regeneration. It is a charm against witchcraft. As a symbol of fertility and prosperity it survives in a decorative form on iron railings. It is also used as a weather oracle. When the cone is hung up in the house it will close when the weather is wet or very cold, and open again when it is dry and hot. In folk lore the pine is a world tree – a sexual symbol where the palm does not flourish. In classical mythology, Attis, a fertile deity, mutilated himself under a pine tree (although another version says he was deprived of his manhood by Agdistis, who was jealous) into which his spirit passed and the tree was bled (cut for turpentine) at the spring equinox. When the tree was cut down it was adorned with ribbons and carried with pomp to the mother goddess' sanctuary, where it was decorated with fleeces and violets. As a phallic symbol it was also dedicated to other fertility deities such as Bacchus, Osiris, Poseidon, Neptune, Dionysus and Pan:

> To Pan was dedicate the pine
> Whose slips the shepherds graceth.

Pine was the established emblem of everything that was considered high and uplifting, and as it was always associated with distant mountains it suggested solitude and a certain dreariness, a theme taken up by poets. Although Shakespeare makes many references to the tree in his plays, it is in *Richard II* that he observes the effect of the rising sun upon a group of pine trees.

> But when from under this terrestrial ball
> He fires the proud top of the eastern Pines.

William Wordsworth also wrote of the pine in a similar context, not, however in the context of his familiar Lake District but when leaving Italy:

My thoughts become bright like yon edging of Pines
On the steep's lofty verge – how it blackened the air!
But touched from behind by the sun, it now shines
With threads that seem part of its own silver hair.

All pines, in what is a large family, yield a resin in varying quantities which is obtained by tapping the tree. The crude resin was almost entirely used for the distillation of oil of turpentine and rosin, only small quantities being used medicinally for ointments and plasters. When oil of turpentine is distilled off, the residue is rosin, but when only part of the oil is extracted it is known as crude turpentine. Oil of turpentine is a good solvent for many resins, wax and fats and was used in making varnish, in oil painting, etc. Medicinally it was used in general and veterinary practice as an antiseptic. For cattle and horses it was used internally as a vermifuge and externally as a stimulant for rheumatic swellings. It was also used for sprains and bruises, and also to kill parasites. Rosin was used for making sealing wax, for resinous soaps for sizing paper, for papier mache and by violinists for rubbing their bows. Tar, which is an impure turpentine, obtained by distillation from the roots of Scots pine, provided an antiseptic and stimulant for veterinary practices and was given to horses with a chronic cough.

PLANE

Put forth thy leaf, thou lofty plane,
East wind and frost are safely gone;
With zephyr mild and balmy rain
The summer comes serenely on;
December days were brief and chill,
The winds of March were wild and drear,
And, nearing and receding still,
Spring never would, we thought, be here.
'In a London Square' A.CLOUGH

PLANE (*Platanus*). The generic name is the Latin word for the tree. The London plane (*platanus x hispanica*) is the species most commonly seen in the city. Plane is not a native or European tree but came from the East. It was often planted and much admired by the Greeks and Romans. Pliny records it growing in France where it is a familiar sight today in every village and hamlet. The name does, however, occur in old vocabularies. Plane trees must have been scarce in the sixteenth century because in 1548, William Turner, author of *A New Herball*, wrote: 'I never saw any Plaine tree In Englande, saving once in Northumberland besyde Morpeth, and an other at Barnwell Abbey besyde Cambryge.' A hundred years later John Evelyn records a special visit to Lee, 'to inspect one as a great curiosity'. Shakespeare however, does make reference to the tree in *Two Noble Kinsmen*:

> *I have sent him where a Cedar,*
> *Higher than all the rest, spreads like a Plane*
> *Fast by a brook.*

According to the *Field Guide of Trees and Shrubs of Britain* the London plane is a hybrid between the western or American

plane, and the eastern or oriental plane.
It was first described in 1670 from a speci-
men growing in Oxford Botanic Gardens, to which it
may have been sent by John Tradescant the younger
(1608–62), gardener to Charles I. Apparently, records
of the Tradescant garden in Lambeth, south London,
show that both planes were growing there. The capability of this handsome and fast growing tree to shed
its bark annually, with its shiny leaves so easily
cleansed by rain, have enabled it to survive the rigours
of pollution generated by city life. A poem, 'London
Trees', by Beryl Netherclift, reflecting earlier times, must
surely have included the plane:

These trees that fling their leafy boughs aloft
In city squares
So little of the ocean-scented winds
And country airs …
Here, in the city's heart
'Neath smoke-hazed skies.
Green trees do their glad part
To lighten country-weary hearts

In plant lore the plane tree is the birthday plant for 24 October
and symbolizes friendliness, genius, magnificence, ornamenta-
tion and shelter. It is the Christian symbol of charity and moral
superiority. The Greeks dedicated the tree to Zeus and the
Romans to Jupiter, pouring libations of wine over its roots.
One source suggests that plane was known to the ancients as
paralisos and was believed to have sprung from the ashes of a
youth of that name who pined to death at the loss of
Melicertes, who with his mother plunged into the sea to escape
the wrath of her husband Athamas. The compassionate gods
transformed them into sea gods. The plane tree under which
the philosophers of Athens sat was known as the Tree of Genius.

PLUM

And sloe and wild plum blossom peeping out
In thickset knotts of flowers preparing gay
For Aprils reign a mockery of May
That soon will glisten on the earnest eye
Like snow white cloaths hung in the sun to drye.
'Shepherd's Calendar' JOHN CLARE

Wild Plum (*Prunus domestica*). The generic name is Latin for plum. The ancestry of the wild plum is somewhat obscure but seems to embrace crosses with blackthorn and various sweeter plum species from Asia in what Richard Mabey referred to as 'a lineage of Byzantine complexity'. Wild plum trees are generally found in hedges and in earlier times were planted as a wind-break for orchards. Since garden plums were first introduced to the English palate their popularity has gone from strength to strength, so much so, that John Gerard remarked that 'to write of Plums particularly would require a peculiar volume ... my selfe have threescore sorts in my garden, and all are strange and rare; there be other places many more common, and yet yearly commeth to our hands others not before knowne.'

Vita Sackville-West gave her advice in 'The Garden':

> *... plant in jewelled swagger, twin with use,*
> *Myrobolans, prolific cherry-plum,*
> *Topaz and ruby, where the bees may hum*
> *In early blossom, and, with summer come,*
> *Children and wasps dispute the wealth of juice.*

In *The Plantlore and Garden Craft of Shakespeare* (1896) H. Ellacombe wrote 'Plums, Damsons and Prunes may conveniently joined together ... Damsons were originally from Damascus and in 1588 were known as Damaske Prunes and considered a great delicacy'. However Shakespeare does not mention the wild plum in his plays although their are various references to the cultivated variety and to prunes, which are the dried fruit, and also to damsons. In *The Merry Wives of Windsor* he wrote:

> *Three veneys for a dish of stewed Prunes.*

And in *Venus and Adonis*:

> *The mellow Plum doth fall, the green sticks fast,*
> *Or, being early pluck'd, is sour to taste.*

And again in *Venus and Adonis*:

> *Like a green Plum that hangs upon a tree,*
> *And falls, through wind, before the fall should be.*

Green plums pickled with vinegar, mustard seed and salt, were very popular some time ago. The fruit 'was gathered before they begin to turn, or before the stone is formed'. Pulling ripe plums can be fraught with danger, as their sweet odour attracts the attention of the tiger-skinned wasp:

> *They were the wasps on plums on Stratford walls,*
> *He stung his fingers, stealing ripened fruit,*
> *No mine or thine,*
> *A schoolboy's loot*

wrote Vita Sackville-West in 'The Garden'. Nevertheless bottled plums and preserves have long been a staple of the country

larder. Their use as a pudding, either stewed or in pies, often resulted in the delightful custom of counting the number of plum stones left on the plate. A girl tried to discover what her future husband would be, when or if they would marry, the type of material for her wedding dress and how she would be transported to the church. This of course resulted in a certain amount of subterfuge!

Who would she marry?

A tinker, tailor, soldier, sailor
Rich man, poor man, beggar man, thief.

Which year?

This year, next year, sometime, never.
The Wedding Dress?
Silk, satin, muslin, rags

Mode of transport?

Coach, carriage, wheelbarrow, muck cart.

Wild plums can be used for culinary purposes and are said to be a sweeter substitute for sloes in alcoholic cordials.

In Wales the early flowering of the plum in December foretold a death in the family. In plant lore wild plum blossom is the birthday flower for 15 June and symbolizes fidelity. In the language of the flowers it means 'Keep your promises.' Herbalists, particularly Culpepper, considered the fruit so well known that it needed no description, and as was his particular custom with all flora, assigned it to a planet: 'all plums belong to Venus and, are, like women, some better and some worse'. He recommended the leaves boiled in wine as 'good to wash and gargle mouth and throat ... or almonds of the ears'. The gum of the tree was prescribed for kidney stones and with leaves boiled in vinegar applied was alleged to 'kill tetters and ringworms.' He also quotes Matthilus, 'the oil pressed out of the kernels of the stones...is good against inflamed piles and tumours or swellings of ulcers, hoarseness, roughness of the tongue and throat, and pains in the ears.' He also mentions the dried fruit, prunes. When stewed they are often used 'in health and sickness to relish the mouth and stomach, to procure appetite, and a little to open the body, allay cholera, and cool the stomach.'

In her poem, 'March', Nora Hopper saw the blooming of the tree as one of the signs of spring:

Blossom on the plum
Wild wind and merry;
Leaves upon the cherry,
And one swallow comes.

Nevertheless, in a year when plum flourishes all else is said to fail, as the old adage suggests:

A plum year
A dumb year.

POMEGRANATE

A little sour is the juice of the pomegranate
Like the juice of unripe raspberries.
Waxlike is the flower
Coloured as the fruit is coloured.
'Ronde de la Grenade' ANDRÉ GIDE

POMEGRANATE (*Pumica granatum*) The botanical name comes from the Old French *pume grenate*, pomegranate apple. The native home of the tree was probably North Africa and it was certainly cultivated in earlier times in Egypt, as it was fondly remembered by the Israelites in their desert wanderings. It grew in abundance in Palestine and is frequently mentioned in the Bible, where it is always an object of beauty and desire. Evidence of this is seen in its selection for the choicest ornaments on the ark of the Tabernacle, on the priests' vestments and on the capitals of the pillars in the Temple of Solomon. It was first cultivated in England prior to 1548, Turner describing it at that time thus: 'Pomegranat trees growe plentuously in

Italy and in Spayne, and there are certayne in my Lorde's gardene at Syon, but their fruite cometh never with perfection.' In 1876 the author naturalist, the Rev Friend recalled 'a tree in Bath with more than sixty fruit; the fruits will perhaps seldom be worth eating, but they are curious and handsome.'

Pomegranates form small, ornamental trees or bushes. Although they are evergreen in the sub-tropics they are deciduous in cooler climates. In summer they have distinctive orange-red flowers. This blossom in plant lore is the birthday flower for 10 June and signifies foolishness and mature elegance. Pomegranate symbolizes concord, fecundity, female principle, immortality, hope, love (pomegranate roots, if separated, twist together again), resurrection, union and virginity. The tree is sometimes thought of as the Tree of Knowledge. In the Christian tradition it represents the church and congregation; a gift which Christ carried down from Heaven, hence God's blessing. It is also an emblem of the Virgin Mary. Depicted on the blue robes of Hebrew high priests it typifies faithfulness. However, if bells are included in the design it indicates lightning and thunder. As the fruit is beautiful at a distance but will not bear close inspection, it is a synonym for persons of fine appearance but of indifferent character. In Greek antiquity it is said to have sprung from the blood of Dionysus, deity of vegetation. Pomegranate is an attribute of Hera, sister-wife of Zeus and of Persephone, daughter of Demeter and Zeus, who was abducted whilst picking daffodils, and taken to Hades; as she had eaten a pomegranate seed she was magically bound to return to her husband periodically and reign as queen of the underworld. Thus the pomegranate was a symbol of death, deity, food and hope for immortality.

> *He takes the cleft pomegranate seeds:*
> *'Love, eat with me this parting day;'*
> *'Demeter's daughter, wouldst away?'*
> *The gates of Hades set her free;*
> *'She will return full soon,' saith he*
> *'My wife, my wife Persephone.'*

Historically the fruit was the heraldic emblem of Henry IV, Moorish king of Grenada who used it with the motto, 'Sour yet sweet' to intimate that a good king should temper severity with mildness (the calyx does resemble a crown). Later it became the device of Catherine of Aragon, the first wife of Henry VIII. It is recorded that in a court masque in her honour, a bank of roses and pomegranates typified the union of Spain and England. Her daughter Mary took the pomegranate and white and red roses as her device. Shakespeare mentions the fruit several times in his plays, including *Romeo and Juliet*:

> *It was the nightingale and not the lark,*
> *That pierced the fearful hollow of thine ear;*
> *Nightly she sings on yon Pomegranate tree.*

The imported fruit of the tree was first used by earlier herbalists. In a Bill of Medicines furnished for the use of Edward 1, pomegranate is listed 'Item pro vino malorum granatorum'. In 1596 John Gerard wrote of 'wine which is pressed forth of the Pomegranate berries named Rhoitas or wine of Pomegranates'. However, he did grow some trees, recording 'I have recovered divers young trees hereof, by sowing of the seed or grains of the height of three or four cubits, attending God's leisure for floures and fruit.' Three years later Butte's *Dyet's Dry Dinner* advised 'if one eate three small Pomegranate flowers (they say) for a whole yeare he shall be safe from all manner of eyesore'. Medicinally the seed within the fruit was said to be soothing and was used with the rind to treat complaints associated with the blood, such as menstruation and spitting blood, whereas the fruit, which is a mild astringent, had a cooling effect on some fevers. It was also used to treat ulcers in the ears and nose, dropsy and a solution extracted from the flowers allegedly fastened loose teeth. The rind was an ingredient in the blackest and most durable ink.

ROWAN

No eye can overlook, when 'mid a grove
Of yet unfaded trees she lifts her head,
Decked with autumnal berries that outshine
Spring's richest blossoms.
'The Mountain Ash' WILLIAM WORDSWORTH

ROWAN *(Sorbus aucuparia)*. The botanical name derives from the Latin, the fruit, and *aucuparias,* for catching birds; fowlers once used the berries as bait to trap game birds. There was no escape for the smaller varieties of birds either, such as thrush, redwing and fieldfares, as they were all destined for the cooking pot. Which explains one of its country names, Fowler's service; it is also known as mountain ash. The common name, rowan or roan, is probably a corruption of *raun,* old Norse for charm, from the tree's alleged power to avert the evil eye. In Scandinavian mythology it is known as Thor's helper or Thor's deliverer, because by clutching a rowan branch he was able to cross the flooded Vimur safely on his way to the Land of the Frost Giants. The protective virtues of the plant against bewitchment were well known throughout Britain:

For witches have no power
Where there is rowan tree wood.

It was believed that rowan tree branches collected on the eve of the Invention of the Cross, a church festival held on 3 May to commemorate the discovery of the Cross by St Helena, would give protection against the influence of witches and other evil spirits. Red thread would sometimes be entwined around the branches which were placed in windows; wells were also dressed to protect their only water source. Similar claims were made for Good Friday, May Day and Holy Rood Day.

Roan-tree and red thread
Haud the witches a'
in dread.

so the old adage goes.
In Scotland, when a
house was built, the
cross beams of the
chimney were often
made from the wood
and on quarter days a
rowan stick was laid
over the door lintel,
both being vulnerable points
for the entry of evil spirits. In some
parts of Britain it was placed in the roof thatch as a protection
against fire. The livestock and farm buildings had to be safe-
guarded and if cattle were thought to have been 'overlooked',
sprays of rowan would be placed above the stalls or over their
horns.

Pigs were often thought to fatten more quickly if a garland
of rowan was hung round the neck. Horse whips, tethering
pegs for cattle, plough pins and churn staffs for making butter
were all fashioned from the wood. A farmer and his wife would
have worn necklaces of rowan and the rockers on their child's
cradle would also have been made of the wood to ensure the
innocence of the child. A final precaution involved planting a
rowan tree near the house to protect the inhabitants. A verse
from an old ballad with the somewhat unusual title of 'The
Laidley Worm of Spindleston Heugghs', reveals the dismay of
the witches on encountering such a tree:

Their spells were in vain. The hags returned
To their queen in sorrowful mood,
Crying that witches have no power
Where thrives the Roan-tree wood

Rowan marked the quickening of the year and the first of the

quarter days on which British witches celebrated their sab-baths. At a time when evil spirits and wraiths occupied the minds of the superstitious it may have been little consolation to know that a rowan stake hammered into the heart of a corpse kept its ghost quiet. The Druids too, venerated the rowan, burning branches to summon spirits to take part in battle. The tree could always be found growing near huge piles of stones associated with their places of worship.

Mountain ash is an appropriate common name, as the tree also grows in some of the highest regions in Britain. Creamy-white clusters of flowers which delight the eye in May, give way in autumn to a colourful splash of scarlet berries, nestled amongst the gloriously autumnal tinted pinnate leaves. Such abundance foretold a poor grain harvest in Scotland.

Mony rains, mony Rowan
Mony Rowans, mony Yewans.

Yewans are a light grain. Next to angelica, rowan was alleged to be the strongest shield against witchcraft, the red berries being of additional value as anything of that colour was abhorrent to witches. Common names reflect this magical association such as witchwood, witchbane, wichen or wish ash. Welsh children called it wiggen, gathering the berries from which their mothers made a sweet liquor. Herbalists used a decoction of the bark in the treatment of diarrhoea and as a vaginal injection for leucorrhoea. The ripe berries, with high vitamin C content, were used to treat scurvy, also as an astringent gargle for sore throats and inflamed tonsils. Today they are made into a delicious jelly which is a popular accompaniment served with game.

In the language of flowers rowan symbolizes beauty, hospitality and protection.

SYCAMORE

The branching sycamore, that veils
His golden sheets in dark-green scales,
While still, as on the fabric goes,
Each pair to each succeeding shows
Its produce in a traverse line,
That step by step they all combine
To frame, by constant interchange,
Of cross like ferns a gradual range.
'Sycamore' BISHOP MANT

SYCAMORE (*Acer pseudoplatanus*). The generic name means sharp in Latin, and refers to the hardness of the wood. It is Europe's largest growing maple and known as the great maple or false plane. The name sycamore was given by earlier botanists in the mistaken belief that the tree was identical to the sycamore or mulberry-fig of Palestine which it resembles in size and foliage. This handsome tree is not indigenous to Great Britain but had probably been introduced by the fifteenth century and has since become naturalized. Planted for its rapid growth it forms effective windbreaks, providing shelter around homes and large buildings, particularly farmsteads, where the coolness of the dairy was an essential priority before refrigeration was invented. The sycamore matures quickly, providing timber within sixty years. The creamy-white wood, which does not warp and is easy to work with was popular in earlier times for making patterns, and because it has no odour to taint food, for household utensils, such as spoons, rolling pins and baking boards. It was also used by saddlers, millwrights and for making kitchen furniture. The more decoratively grained pieces were reserved for musical instruments and veneers. The scimitar shaped winged seeds, known as keys, or 'helicopters' in

England and 'backies' in Scotland, are used in flying competitions and model making. The young trees are often infested with honeydew which makes the sycamore tree unsuitable for planting near paths and on lawns. However William Wordsworth had fond recollections of the tree in the poem 'Guilt and Sorrow':

> *The staff I well remember which upbore*
> *The bending body of my active sire;*
> *His seat beneath the honied sycamore*
> *Where the bees hummed, and chair by winter fire.*

Coleridge also noted the harmonious sounds of the insects in his 'Inscription For A Fountain':

> *This Sycamore, oft musical with bees,*
> *Such tents the Patriarchs loved*
> *O long unharmed May all its aged boughs o'er canopy*
> *The small round basin, which this jutting stone*
> *Keeps pure from falling leaves.*

Robert Louis Stevenson (1850–94), in 'Envoy', obviously regarded the presence of a sycamore near the home amongst the pleasures of a contented life:

> *Go, little book, and wish to all*
> *Flowers in the garden, meat in the hall*
> *A bin of wine, a spice of wit,*
> *A house with lawns enclosing it,*
> *A living river by the door,*
> *A nightingale in the sycamore!*

The dense foliage and heavy lower branches of a mature tree provide a welcome refuge on a warm day, and sycamores were often planted for this reason as shade-trees on village greens and in parks and gardens. Shakespeare was mindful of their usefulness in *Love's Labour's Lost*:

> *Under the cool shade of a Sycamore*
> *I thought to close mine eyes some half-hour*

and also in *Othello*:

> *The poor soul sat sighing by a*
> *Sycamore tree.*

That they were often planted in groups is evident in *Romeo and Juliet*:

> *Underneath the grove of Sycamore*
> *That westward rooteth from the city's side,*
> *So early did I see your son.*

In the Scottish Highlands a good wine is said to have been produced from the sap; the tree trunks were pierced in the autumn and spring and the sap fermented with the addition of sugar. The dried leaves were used as sheep fodder. In *Plant-Lore and Garden Craft of Shakespeare* the large syca-more is said to have served a different purpose in the west of Scotland where it was called dool or grief tree, as 'they were used by powerful barons for hanging their enemies and refractory vassals on.'

The book also noted that there was one yet 'standing on the River Doon. It was used by the family of Kennedy, who were the most powerful barons of the West of Scotland.'

In plant lore sycamore is the birthday emblem for 1 July and symbolizes grief, curiosity and truth. It is the Christian symbol of the cross (Peter of Capua), cupidity (Saint Melitus), unbelieving Jew (Rhaban Maur) and wisdom (Saint Euchre). There are many surviving landmark trees in England from art, literature and history, each with their own folklore. They range from those mentioned by Emily Brontë in *Wuthering Heights*, which can be seen today by tourists visiting the moorland near Howarth in Yorkshire, to the Belfry Tree at Dulverton, Somerset and the Posy Tree at Mapperton in Devon, where a plaque reads: 'It was past this tree that the local victims of the great plague were carried to a common grave by the surviving villagers'. The Poo Hill Tree was used as a landmark on the pack-horse way near Huddersfield in Yorkshire and the Wishing Tree on Helm Common, Kendal also remains. A sad

story is told of the
sycamore on Matlock
in Derbyshire. Two
young brothers
each planted a
sycamore on top
of the hill,
which they hoped
to see grow into large
trees. Only one tree
survived and this is
said to have reflected
their future, as only
one was successful.
Another version says that
like the tree, he died. The
Martyrs' Tree on the Green
at Tolpuddle, Dorset, is the
sycamore under which dis-
satisfied local farm workers
met to discuss their griev-
ances in the 1830s. It is regarded
as the birthplace of the first agricultural trade union. Of the six men that
were subsequently deported, one, the
leader George Loveless, is said to have taken a leaf from the
tree, pressed between the pages of his Bible. On the 150th
anniversary of the deportation, Len Murray, then General
Secretary of the Trades Union Congress, planted a seedling
from the tree a few yards away on the Green.

TAMARISK

High noon behind the talarisks – the sun is hot above us –
As at the Home the Christmas day is breaking wan.
They will drink our healths at dinner – those who
*   tell us how they love us*
And forget us till another year be gone!
'Christmas in India' RUDYARD KIPLING

TAMARISK (*Tamarix anglica*). This ornamental shrub which can grow to tree size, attaining heights of ten feet, was named after the Tamarisci, who inhabited the banks of the Tamaris, known as the Tambra, in Spain, where it grew in abundance, although it flourishes in the Middle East. This may account for the suggestion that the name is derived from the Hebrew *tamaris*, meaning broom – the flexible twiggy branches are well adapted for this purpose. In his *Pastorals* Browne records such a domestic use:

> *Amongst the rest, Tamarisk there stood*
> *For housewives besoms onely knowe most good.*

Pliny also mentions the use the Romans made of the tree as a broom. Homer, among others, refers to the tamarisk as the tree by which Achilles laid his spear before he rushed into Xanthus, the campsite, in pursuit of the fleeing Trojans.

> *So plunged in Xanthus, by Achilles' force*
> *Roars the resounding surge with men and horse;*
> *His bloody lance the hero cast aside,*
> *Which spreading Tamarisk on them margins hide.*

The trees that grow in the Middle East are a larger variety and are highly prized for their medicinal qualities, and for a honey-like substance obtained from the branches. The wood was also used as fuel and for drinking vessels – it supplied a variety of needs for the nomadic Bedouin tribes. In ancient times the fine twigs had a more unusual role – they were bound round the heads of criminals – a marked contrast to an old Cornish way of making lobster-pots. Being resistant to salt in the atmosphere, the tamarisk grows well around coastal areas of Britain where it often colonizes sand dunes.

Wind sways pink of Summer
Tamarisk against the blue
Drowsy, after an indigestive night
I point this out to you

wrote G. Grigson in 'August near the Beauce'. Tamarisk grows wild on the south and east coasts, contorted and fashioned by the prevailing winds where it also helps to stabilize the shingle beaches. As the alternate leaves are so numerous and small they give a feathery appearance to the foliage, a delightful foil for the dainty pink or white flowers in midsummer. In milder areas one may be fortunate enough to see it flowering until Christmas, a magical touch to the garden in winter.

In plant lore tamarisk is the birthday flower for 8 October and symbolizes crime. Culpepper assigned it to the planet Saturn, describing it 'as so well known that it needs no description'. The root, leaves and young branches, or bark boiled in wine and drunk had his recommendation for 'bleeding haemorrhoidal veins, spitting blood, jaundice, colic, the biting of all venomous serpents, except the asp, and the too abounding of women's courses.' A decoction for external use was used for toothache and earache, for red and watering eyes, with honey added, for 'gangrenous and fretting ulcers' and, with surprising diversity, to wash 'those that are subject to lice.'

Some sources suggest that the tamarisk was first introduced to Cornwall. However, the Rev Thomas Fuller (1608–61) in *Worthies of England* suggests that the tamarisk was brought over from Switzerland by Dr Edmund Grindal, Bishop of London, during the reign of Elizabeth I; he had been in exile under Queen Mary. It is said to have first grown in his physic garden at Fulham where at that time 'The soil being moist and fenny, well complied with the nature of this plant; yet it groweth not up to be timber, as in Arabia, though often to that substance that cups of great size are made thereof.' The reference to cups is significant as in those days such a receptacle made of tamarisk was thought to improve the flavour of ale. Similarly a tamarisk spit, on which meat was roasted 'could only add to the excellence'. Physicians further increased the popularity of the wood by advising their patients to eat from dishes carved from tamarisk reflecting its medicinal use in ancient times.

WALNUT

How have I wearied with many a stroke
The stately Walnut tree, the while the rest
Under the tree fell all for nuts at strife:
For ylike to me was libertee and lyfe.
'The Shepheardes Calender' EDMUND SPENSER

WALNUT (*Juglans regia*). The generic name is from the Latin
Jovis (Jupiter) and *glans*, acorn – literally, Jupiter's nut. The
name is said to be derived from the 'golden age' when men
lived on acorns and the gods upon walnuts. It was introduced
into Italy from Persia and was known as the Persian or Royal
Nut. Highly valued as a food and cooking oil it was mentioned
growing there by Varr (born BC 116). In all probability it was
brought to Britain as seed by the Romans and was simply called
Nut. The English name is partly German in origin and simply
means foreign or non-English nut. Some say it was introduced
in 1561 but Gerard, writing about thirty years later, mentions
the tree being very common in fields near highways and in
orchards. Nevertheless the walnut tree was firmly established in
Shakespeare's time. Writers of the day spoke of it as a high and
large tree and the bard mentions it too, in *The Taming of the
Shrew*:

Why, 'tis a cockle or a Walnut-shell,
A knack, a toy, a trick, a baby's cap.

And also in *The Merry Wives of Windsor*:

Let them say of me, 'As jealous as Ford that searched a hollow
Walnut for his wife's leman'

Some consideration was given to the planting of the tree as it
was believed there was antipathy between apples and walnuts.

In *History of Cultivated Vegetables* Phillips wrote of the apple
tree as:

> *Uneasy seated by funeral Yew*
> *Or Walnut (whose malignant touch impairs*
> *All generous fruits), or near the bitter dews*
> *Of Cherries*

Walnut was also considered to be an enemy of the oak and if
planted together, it was said, one would not survive the winter.
An old saying refers to its slow growth:

> *Who plants a walnut tree expects not to eat the fruit.*

Ensuring a successful harvest, however, prompted an old saying:

> *A woman and a spaniel and a walnut tree,*
> *The more you beat them, the better they be.*

An alternative version substitutes steak for spaniel. Marks on
old trees show evidence of past treatment which was administered with a bill-hook in early March, when the sap is rising.
Fully grown green nuts gathered on a sunny day in July were
used in recipes for pickled walnuts; an eighteenth century one
suggests soaking them in salted water for 'nine days, stir them
twice a day, and change the water every three days; then place

them on a hair sieve and let them remain in the air until they turn black; put them in stone jars and let them stand until cold, then boil the vinegar three-times, pour it over the walnuts, and let it become cold between each boiling; tie them down with a bladder and let them stand three months'. A pickle consisting of two quarts of vinegar, two ounces each of mace, cloves, black pepper, Jamaica pepper, ginger and long pepper plus two ounces of salt, boiled for ten minutes was poured hot on the walnuts and sealed with paper and a bladder. Walnut ketchup, the recipe consisting basically of a hundred green nuts, shallots, garlic, salt, vinegar, anchovies, pepper and mace, was also popular. Walnut vinegar, which required the green shells to be soaked for fourteen days in 'salt and water, sufficiently strong to bear an egg', drained, and dried in the sun for nine days, then put in stone jars and topped with boiling vinegar, was another favourite.

The timber of the walnut was highly prized for furniture and gun-stocks and the oil, according to the preface in *Arts of the Middle Ages*, highly valued 'as it allows the artist as much time as he requires in order to blend his colours and finish his work'. In conjunction with amber varnish it forms a vehicle which leaves nothing to be desired, and which doubtless was the vehicle of Van Eyck, and in many instances of the Venetian masters, and of Correggio. During the nineteenth century the oil was used in the manufacture of soap. The fragrant leaves were recommended as a constituent of pot-pourri and as a decoction for killing slugs.

Walnut is the birthday plant for 15 March and symbolizes intellect, longevity, presentiment and stratagem. A walnut branch signifies contagion. The black walnut (*Juglans nigra*) symbolizes strength and tenacity. Medieval witches were said to gather beneath its branches. White walnut (*Juglans cinerea*) signifies lack of dignity, explained by the tree's cragginess and sparse foliage. The tree is also sacred to the Roman god, Jupiter. In Greek and Roman antiquity the walnut is a symbol of fertility and was served at wedding celebrations. Astrologically the tree is assigned to the sun.

WILD CHERRY

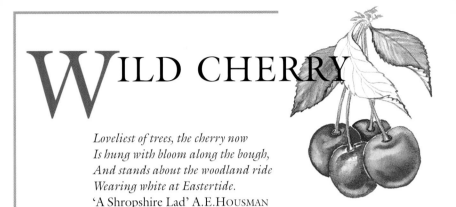

Loveliest of trees, the cherry now
Is hung with bloom along the bough,
And stands about the woodland ride
Wearing white at Eastertide.
'A Shropshire Lad' A.E.HOUSMAN

WILD CHERRY (*Prunus avium*). The generic name is Latin for plum. Wild cherry is also known as gean, mazzard and murry. The small but attractive fruit, in varying shades of red through to yellow – colours repeated in a stunning autumnal leaf display – are rather thin-fleshed, but provide a welcome source of food for birds, as well as mice and squirrels (if the evidence of small piles of cherry stones is to be believed). As with other fruit trees, the wild cherry has been crossed and selected to produce better fruiting varieties such as the Morello, May Duke and Kentish cherries. A cultivated cherry is said to have been introduced from Flanders during the reign of Henry VIII although the first recorded orchard was New Garden, which Michael Drayton (1562–1631) refers to in his 'Polyolbion':

When Thames-ward to the shore which shoots upon the rise,
Rich Tenham undertakes thy closeits to suffice
With cherries which we say the summer in doth bring
Wherewith Pomona crowns the young and lustful Spring,
Whose golden gardens seem the Hesperides to mock,
Nor where the damson wants, nor dainty Apricock.

Wild cherry, which is not particularly palatable, was used for making summer pies and as an alternative to the Morello as the main ingredient for cherry brandy. An earthenware jar was packed with the fruit and sprinkled with crushed brown sugar, topped with brandy and tied down with a bladder.

In plant lore cherry blossom signifies spiritual beauty. In the language of the flowers it means: 'Do me justice'. A single blossom means education and a double blossom false hope. The tree symbolizes Great Divine Spirit but also truth – recalling the George Washington legend of the boy that never told a lie. A white cherry tree signifies deception. The fruit of the tree symbolizes increase, merry-making and virginity. It typifies the generative power of nature. In the Christian tradition it indicates delights of the blessed and fruit of paradise; one legend tells of Jesus giving St Peter a cherry and chiding him gently not to scorn small things.

In folklore the cherry is associated with the cuckoo. The reason seems to stem from a strange belief that the bird must eat three good meals of cherries before he is allowed to stop singing. On hearing the first call of the bird in spring superstitious adults thought it prudent to turn over the money in their pocket for luck, saying:

Cuckoo, cherry tree
Catch a penny and give it to me.

Children would shake a cherry tree when it was in blossom and chant:

Cuckoo, cherry tree
Good bird tell me
How many years before I die.

The number of 'cuckoos' in the bird's call gave them the answer. Cherry stones, which are the hard seed of the cherry, were used to count one's fortune in the following years, when the fruit was eaten in a pie. In the children's game of cherry-pit, in which the cherry stones are thrown into a small hole, the same legend applied. William Shakespeare makes reference to it in *Twelfth Night*:

What, man! 'tis not for gravity to play at cherry-pit with
Satan; hang him, foul collier

In 'The Choice' Katharine Tynan wrote:.

> *Cherries in nets against the wall,*
> *Where master thrush his madrigal*
> *Sings, and makes oath, a churl is he*
> *Who grudges cherries for a fee.*

The fruit was grown commercially in the orchards of Kent where farmers also used the ground to graze sheep. Charles Dickens noted in *Pickwick Papers*, 'Kent! Sir – everybody knows Kent – apples, cherries, hops and women.' Families of fruit pickers made annual expeditions and fruit sales, known as cherry fairs, were held. These gatherings frequently developed into boisterous parties. However, from their temporary character they came to typify the evanescence of life; thus John Gower said of this world 'Alle is but a cherye-fayre', meaning that it is simply a passing show that will not last.

In poetry the fruit is often associated with feminine lips and cheeks. Shakespeare made several references, including 'With Cherry lips, and cheeks of damask roses' in *Two Noble Kinsmen* and in *A Midsummer Night's Dream*:

> *O, how ripe in show*
> *Thy lips. those kissing Cherries, tempting grow.*

> *Cherry-ripe, ripe, ripe, I cry,*
> *Full and fair ones; come and buy:*
> *If so be, you ask me where*
> *They do grow? I answer, there,*
> *Where my Julia's lips do smile*
> *There's the land, or cherry-isle.*

Herbalists used gum extracted from the tree, dissolved in wine, as a syrup for coughs and sore throats. Children and foresters also picked this substance, which exudes from the tree when damaged, as a bitter-sweet chewing gum. Cherry wood is a beautiful colour and makes fine furniture. The shiny chestnut-coloured bark peels off in horizontal strips, and is used for veneers.

WILLOW

WILLOW (*Salix*). The generic name, *salix*, is Latin for willow and probably derives from two Celtic words, *sal* and *lis*, meaning near water. Willow is derived from the Old English *wilig*, *welige* and *withig*, signifying a plant suitable for withes or ties – the flexible twigs were widely used in basketwork and finer types of wickerwork. James Graham wrote:

To name the uses of the Willow tribe
Were endless tasks. The baskets various forms
For various purposes of household thrift,
The wicker chair, of size and shape antique,
The rocking couch of sleeping infancy

The native large willow family and their variety of names can be very confusing but one thing they have in common is their habitat: banks of streams, rivers and damp places. Probably the most familiar are the sallows (*salix caprea*) with their beautiful catkins, also known as pussy willow, goat willow, sally withy, palm and saugh tree palmer (a palmer was a person who had been to the Holy Land). In earlier times it was used in Palm Sunday processions – probably because it was in flower – to represent the true palm leaves strewn along the way when Jesus rode into Jerusalem. Goethe (1749–1832) wrote of the festival:

In Rome upon Palm Sunday
They bear true palms:
The Cardinals bow reverently,

And sing old 'psalms';
Elsewhere their psalms are sung
'Mid olive branches,
The holly bough supplies their places
Among the avalanches
More Northern climes must be content
With the sad willow.

Today it is still associated with the festival of Easter when it decorates church and home. Children used to wear sprigs of pussy willow on Palm Sunday; if not, they were likely to get their hair pulled. In the north of England a seemingly more drastic custom is said to have taken place. Branches of the pussy willow were shaped in the form of St Andrew's Cross with catkins or blossom at each point and bound together with ribbon. This gave rise to the saying 'He that hath not a Palm in his hand on Palm Sunday must have his hand cut off.' The crosses were then hung on the cottage walls for the remainder of the year. Small natural palm crosses, a delightful relic of the past, are still given by the priest to the congregation in some parts of the country. Willow may have been chosen because it was one of the plants used by the Israelites to celebrate the feast of the Tabernacle: 'they were to gather the boughs of goodly tree, branches of palm, and the boughs of thick trees and willow of the brook and to rejoice before the Lord their God seven days.' It was also the willow upon which the Jews hung their harps when they sat down and wept in remembrance of their native land. In Christianity the willow signifies Christ's Gospel.

The white willow (*Salix alba*) was pollarded by our ancestors, giving a regular crop of small poles which were used for fencing, basket work and kindling. Many of the trees have now disappeared, partly due to mechanical drainage methods; the loss of the binding root systems has contributed to the erosion of the banks of ditches and streams. In East Anglia a cultivated variety is grown to supply wood for cricket bats. Weeping willow (*Salix x chrysocoma*) is a popular ornamental tree gracing gardens, lakes and river banks with its cascade of fine branches sweeping to the ground. Some writers thought they drooped mournfully, suggesting that the long narrow leaves resembled tears; in mythology the willow is sacred to Circe, Hecate and Persephone, all death aspects of the mother goddess, and consequently it became a symbol of mourning. Astrologically all willows are assigned to the moon and in plant lore it is the birthday flower for 22 May, symbolizing celibacy and forsaken love:

> *A Willow garland thou didst send*
> *Perfumed, last day, to me*
> *Which did but only this portend*
> *I was forsook by thee*

wrote Robert Herrick. Shakespeare also refers to this symbolism on several occasions, for example in *Much Ado About Nothing*:

> *I offered him my company to a Willow tree, either to make*
> *him a garland, as being forsaken, or to bind him up a*
> *rod, as being worthy to be whipped.*

A spray of willow worn in the hat was also a sign of a rejected lover. The weeping willow is the birthday flower for 21 May and symbolizes sadness and mourning. It is a funeral tree signifying coming sorrow. Water willow is the birthday flower for 4 July, symbolizing freedom and French willow is the birthday flower for 3 December, symbolizing constancy. Creeping willow signifies disappointed love.

Osier (*Salix viminalis*) is the willow that is coppiced – cut down once a year to ground level – so that it grows long pliant stems, or 'withies', which are steamed and dried and the bark left on, for brown willow. To make buff willow the shoots are boiled and the bark stripped off, whereas white willow can only be prepared in the spring after winter storage in water.

> *The building thrush watches old Job who stacks*
> *The bright-peeled osiers on the sunny fence*

wrote Edmund Blunden in 'The Poor Man's Pig'. Formerly osier was in great demand for lobster pots, fish-traps, chairs, baskets and numerous household items.

> *For first an osier colender provide*
> *Of twigs thick wrought: such toiling peasants twine,*
> *When through streight passages they strein their wine.*

Fortunately withy-growing is still practised today but on a much smaller scale, meeting the increasing demand for hand-crafted articles. A traditional dance known as 'strip the willow' owes its name to the 'peeling off' movement of the dancers. In plant lore, osier is the birthday flower for 3 July and symbolizes frankness.

During the Middle Ages willow was believed to be a giver of eloquence and was sacred to poets. It was also used as a means of love divination – after running round the house three times holding a willow wand a girl would see her future husband grasping the end of the stick. However, beating a child with a willow stick was thought to stunt its growth – because the willow decays early.

Herbalists recommended the burnt ashes of willow bark mixed with vinegar for the treatment of warts and a concoction of leaves or bark in wine, rinsed through the hair as a satisfactory cure for dandruff. In *Brevairie of Health* (1598) the oils of water lily, rose and willow are recommended for cramp. The tonic and astringent combination was said to render it useful for those recovering from 'acute worms, in chronic diarrhoea and dysentery'. Culpepper, however, used the leaves, bark and seed 'to staunch bleeding, and other fluxes of blood and to stay vomiting and provocation thereunto, if the decoction of them in wine be drunk'. He added: 'the leaves bruised with pepper and drunk with wine, cures windy colic'. He also claimed that bruised leaves boiled in wine subdued lust in man and woman and that the seed had a similar effect – a refreshing alternative from the eternal search for a love potion! He concludes his observation on the willow with the suggestion that 'it is a fine cooling tree, the boughs of which are very convenient to be placed in the chamber of one sick of fever.' Today, experiments continue with extracts of willow bark, as a medical alternative to aspirin.

YEW

YEW (*Taxus Baccata*). The generic name is the Latin word for the tree. The common name is derived from the Old English *iw*, signifying its evergreen nature. With its dark green foliage yew displays tiny green female flowers and yellow male ones which are borne on separate trees and contrast with the attractive, small scarlet fruits of the female species of this native tree. The oldest recorded yew, of which living fragments remain, is in Perthshire, Scotland, and is possibly 2,000 years old. However, after five centuries yews generally begin to lose their heart wood and eventually their hollowed girths need support. These gothic trees are a familiar sight in almost every churchyard and much speculation has been generated about the many reasons and legends associated with this fact. It would seem that in earlier times two yew trees were invariably planted, one near the path, probably to shelter a funeral cortege or assembling congregation, and the other as a possible evergreen canopy in the burial area to protect the mortal remains of the more important parishioners. In later years it became acceptable for local dignitaries to be buried in the body of the church. A pair of yew trees can sometimes be seen at the entrance to a churchyard, often divided by a lych-gate where a coffin would await the arrival of the clergy.

In Greek antiquity such trees represented the celestial twins.

In *Twelfth Night* Shakespeare suggests the deathly association with the tree:

> *My shroud of white, stuck all with yew,*
> *O: prepare it.*

A further explanation for the presence of yew trees in churchyards may have its root in pagan times. Many mythologies believed the yew was a sacred tree and was thus planted in places of worship. In Britain, early Christians, led by Augustine, attempted to convert pagans to what they considered to be a more civilized religion but they retained many of the temples and groves of trees. However, they purified the sites and gradually built their own churches. They accepted and sometimes adapted the many floral offerings associated with the beliefs of their converts, often by adding, as they were Roman Catholics, the prefix 'Our Lady'. Paganism gradually faded into the mists of time. The Druids in particular favoured, along with oak, the yew tree.

The old tradition of decorating graves with evergreens probably dates from the Roman occupation when yew was a substitute for their more familiar cypress. Ancient people would not sit under the shade of the tree (where nothing grows) or even place their beehives nearby in case the bees sucked in its poison. The bark is poisonous, as are cut branches, although cattle sometimes graze on living foliage. The seed of the red berries is also harmful. Perhaps because it is so attractive, the female yew (the sex of a tree being an unknown quantity in earlier times) always seems to be planted overhanging pathways where the fruit could be trodden on. Trees planted at the south-west corner of houses and in churchyards were regarded as potent protection against evil spirits. Nevertheless a sprig of yew stolen from a churchyard at the appropriate time was thought to be an excellent ingredient for a magic potion, as Shakespeare noted in *Macbeth*. The witches included one in their brew, along with the more indigestible newts, wool of bat, toe of frog and tongue of dog:

Slips of yew
Sliver'd in the moon's eclipse

Although cutting down and burning a yew tree was said to be very unlucky they were highly prized in the Middle Ages for making longbows. The ones made from consecrated yew from a churchyard were considered to be of higher value. During the reign of Edward IV every Englishman and Irishman living in England was commanded to have 'a bow of his height made of Yew, Wych-hazel of Awburne'. Nevertheless the finest bows were made of yew wood imported from Italy and Spain. Several English kings have died as a result of the bow, including Harold, William Rufus and Richard the Lionheart.

What of the bow?
The bow was made in England:
Of true wood, of yew wood,
The yew of English bows

wrote Arthur Conan Doyle in 'Song of the Bow'. John Keats furnishes his 'Endymion' with such a bow:

Again I'll poll
The fair-grown Yew tree for a chosen bow.

The noble yew is regarded by some as not only the 'aristocrat of hedges' but the ideal evergreen for the art of topiary, both much in evidence in gardens large and small. In her long poem 'The Garden', Vita Sackville-West writes of the 'slavish gardeners of richy men who through the years the patient yew maltreat':

To such caprice as takes the gardener's mind
In topiary elaborate
Of Pliny's Tuscan villa, or the state
Or royal palace and of country-seat,
As chessmen, dragons, elephants resigned
To carry howdahs; obelisks most near,
Pyramids mocking Egypt, cannon-balls
For ever static on their verdant walls.

In Greek legend the yew was formerly the nymph Smilax who rejected the advances of the youth Crocus. The gods took pity on him and changed him into a flower and her into a tree. Yew is the birthday flower for 20 February and symbolizes death, sadness, immortality and resurrection.

Earlier physicians and herbalists make no mention of possible curative powers of the tree although in recent times research has been undertaken into the medicinal value of an alkaloid, taxol, extracted from yew clippings, as a treatment for ovarian cancer.

In October 1996 the Yews for the Millennium, created by The Conservation Foundation, was launched to provide every parish in the country with a young yew tree propagated from an ancient yew, which was possibly growing at the time of the birth of Christ.

The Laughing Leaves

Wind-tossed long as they live, the trees
Are jubilant communities.
Why do you laugh, O gentle leaves?
The grain is all bound up in sheaves,
And you yourselves are sere and brown,
And here and there one flutters down
To be forever lost to all
Your merriment, to robin's call,
Yet still you laugh as when the May
First kissed you, waxen, glossy, green,
And you unworn by time, were seen.
Are you but laughing leaves at man,
Who knows you not and never can
Until he quits the sorry round
Of loving things that are but found
To be of dross – when at the last
The bubbles of his life are past,
And age betrays? Ah yes, you hold
The secrets of true mirth, and, old
Or young, rejoice, content to feel
Time makes no wound he does not heal.

CHARLES G. BLUNDEN